SHANGHAI
ENCOUNTER

CHRISTOPHER PITTS

Shanghai Encounter

Published by Lonely Planet Publications Pty Ltd
ABN 36 005 607 983

Australia (Head Office)	Locked Bag 1, Footscray, Vic 3011 ☎ 03 8379 8000 fax 03 8379 8111 talk2us@lonelyplanet.com.au
USA	150 Linden St, Oakland, CA 94607 ☎ 510 250 6400 toll free 800 275 8555 fax 510 893 8572 info@lonelyplanet.com
UK	2nd fl, 186 City Rd London EC1V 2NT ☎ 020 7106 2100 fax 020 7106 2101 go@lonelyplanet.co.uk

This edition of *Shanghai Encounter* was written by
Christopher Pitts. Damian Harper wrote the previous
edition. This title was commissioned in Lonely Planet's
Oakland office and produced by: **Commissioning
Editor** Emily K Wolman **Coordinating Editor** Jessica
Crouch **Coordinating Cartographer** Peter Shields
Layout Designer Wibowo Rusli **Assisting Editors**
Kate Evans, Robyn Loughnane, Dianne Schallmeiner,
Saralinda Turner **Assisting Cartographer** Csanad
Csutoros **Managing Editor** Laura Stansfeld **Managing
Cartographer** David Connolly **Cover Research** Dan
Baird, lonelyplanetimages.com **Internal Image
Research** Sabrina Dalbesio, lonelyplanetimages.com
Project Manager Chris Love **Managing Layout
Designer** Laura Jane **Thanks to** Lucy Birchley, Sally
Darmody, Yvonne Kirk, Ji Yuanfang, Rebecca Lalor,
Raphael Richards

ISBN 978 1 74179 411 3

Printed through Colorcraft Ltd, Hong Kong.
Printed in China.

Mixed Sources
Product group from well-managed
forests and other controlled sources
www.fsc.org Cert no. SGS-COC-005002
© 1996 Forest Stewardship Council

HOW TO USE THIS BOOK
Colour-Coding & Maps
Colour-coding is used for symbols on maps and in
the text that they relate to (eg all eating venues on
the maps and in the text are given a green knife and
fork symbol). Each neighbourhood also gets its own
colour, and this is used down the edge of the page
and throughout that neighbourhood section.

Shaded yellow areas on the maps denote areas
of interest — for their historical significance, their
attractive architecture or their great bars and restaurants. We encourage you to head to these areas
and just start exploring!

Prices
Multiple prices listed with reviews (eg Y10/5 or
Y10/5/20) indicate adult/child, adult/concession
or adult/child/family.

Send us your feedback We love to hear from
readers — your comments help make our books better. We read every word you send us, and we always
guarantee that your feedback goes straight to the
appropriate authors. The most useful submissions are
rewarded with a free book. To send us your updates
and find out about Lonely Planet events, newsletters
and travel news visit our award-winning website:
lonelyplanet.com/contact.

Note: We may edit, reproduce and incorporate
your comments in Lonely Planet products such as
guidebooks, websites and digital products, so let us
know if you don't want your comments reproduced or
your name acknowledged. For a copy of our privacy
policy visit *lonelyplanet.com/privacy*.

CHRISTOPHER PITTS

A Philadelphia native, Chris started off his university years studying classical Chinese poetry before a week in 1990s Shanghai (en route to school in Kunming) abruptly changed his focus to the idiosyncrasies of modern China. After spending several years in Asia memorising Chinese characters, he abruptly traded it all in and moved to Paris, where he currently lives with his family: Perrine, Elliot and Céleste. Chris works as a freelance writer, editor and translator for a number of publishers, including University of California Press, and has contributed to several Lonely Planet titles. Visit his website at www.christopherpitts.net.

CHRISTOPHER'S THANKS

Thanks to Damian Harper, author of the stellar 1st edition, and Daniel McCrohan, coauthor of the *Shanghai City Guide*. In Shanghai, thanks to Claudio Valsecchi, Gerald Neumann, Zane Mellupe, Antonio Jiménez Rosa, Munson Wu and Maria Chao. Finally, gratitude to the family on both sides of the Atlantic and kisses to Perrine, Elliot and Céleste.

THE PHOTOGRAPHER

Greg Elms has been a contributor to Lonely Planet for more than 15 years. Armed with a Bachelor of Arts in photography, Greg was a photographer's assistant for two years before embarking on a travel odyssey. He eventually settled down to a freelance career in Melbourne, and now works regularly for magazines, graphic designers, advertising agencies and, of course, publishers such as Lonely Planet.

Our readers Many thanks to the travellers who wrote to us with helpful hints, useful advice and interesting anecdotes. Irene Arriaza, Mark Broadhead, Penny Lattey.

Cover photograph Flying a kite and cycling at sunrise on the Bund, Anthony Arendt/Alamy. **Internal photographs** p45, p57, p76, p89, p95 by Christopher Pitts; p8 Radius Images/Corbis; p87 Bali Laguna; p114 Sunmdm/Dreamstime; p119 Jia Shanghai; p128 Dragonfly Therapeutic Retreat; p132 Giles Robberts/Alamy. All other photographs by Lonely Planet Images and by Greg Elms, except p4, p23, p25 Richard I'Anson; p11 Keren Su; p20 Brent Winebrenner; p30, p39, p116, p135 Phil Weymouth; p47 Martin Puddy; p51 Krzysztof Dydynski; p112 Bruce Bi; p115 John Banagan; p125 Tony Burns.

All images are copyright of the photographers unless otherwise indicated. Many of the images in this guide are available for licensing from **Lonely Planet Images:** lonelyplanetimages.com

Shoppers enjoy a colourful day out

CONTENTS

THE AUTHOR	03
THIS IS SHANGHAI	07
HIGHLIGHTS	08
SHANGHAI DIARY	25
ITINERARIES	29
NEIGHBOURHOODS	34
>THE BUND & PEOPLE'S SQUARE	38
>OLD TOWN	54
>FRENCH CONCESSION EAST	62
>FRENCH CONCESSION WEST	72
>JING'AN	82
>PUDONG	92
>XUJIAHUI & SOUTH SHANGHAI	98
>HONGKOU & NORTH SHANGHAI	104
EXCURSIONS TO CLASSICAL CHINA	109
SNAPSHOTS	116
> ACCOMMODATION	118
> ARCHITECTURE	120
> FOOD	122
> DRINKING	124
> FASHION	126
> SILK & ANTIQUES	127
> MASSAGE & SPA TREATMENT	128
> TAICHI & CHINESE MARTIAL ARTS	129
> ART GALLERIES	130
> MARKETS	131
> CLUBS	132
> GAY & LESBIAN SHANGHAI	133
> RELIGION	134
BACKGROUND	135
DIRECTORY	143
INDEX	155

THIS IS SHANGHAI

There's no place in China quite like Shanghai.
There are no summer palaces, fog-enmeshed
temples or transcendent cliff-side Buddhas here.

Remnants of an alluring past remain, but to dwell there would be to miss
the point entirely. Shanghai has never been about what has already hap-
pened; it is about what is going to happen. For millions of Chinese, it is
more than just a city; it is a symbol of change, opportunity and sophistication. While Beijing may pull the country's strings, Shanghai is the
pacesetter when it comes to future aspirations. It revels in its glamorous
airs and entrepreneurial flair, in its global reach and ability to synthesise
and adapt foreign ideas to home-grown tastes.

Now two decades in the making, the post-Communist megalopolis
is an ever-evolving cityscape. Old Concession architecture stands in the
shadows of giant towers, glitzy restaurants open around the corner from
tiny dumpling stands, and the intermittent flashes of welding torches
compete with neon signs and ubiquitous TV screens. More than any
other place in the Middle Kingdom, Shanghai is electrified with youthful
optimism and prospects. Business may be the city's raison d'être, but
there's plenty to do here, from nonstop shopping and skyscraper hopping to stand-out art and fantastic eats.

As modern China's ground zero, the city exudes a unique style that's
unlike anywhere else in the country. Often portrayed as a blend of East
and West, Shanghai, with its voracious appetite for new styles and trends,
is above all cosmopolitan and cutting edge. It's a place to taste a future
that's just around the bend, to hang on to the roller-coaster ride of
change, to hunt down the ghosts of old alleyways, the vanishing remains
of debauched glory days and the creations of the next generation. For
deal makers, fashion freaks, in-the-know foodies and those who just want
to ride the crest of China's emerging wave – this is Shanghai.

Left Hearty homestyle meals at Dongbei Ren (p69)

>HIGHLIGHTS

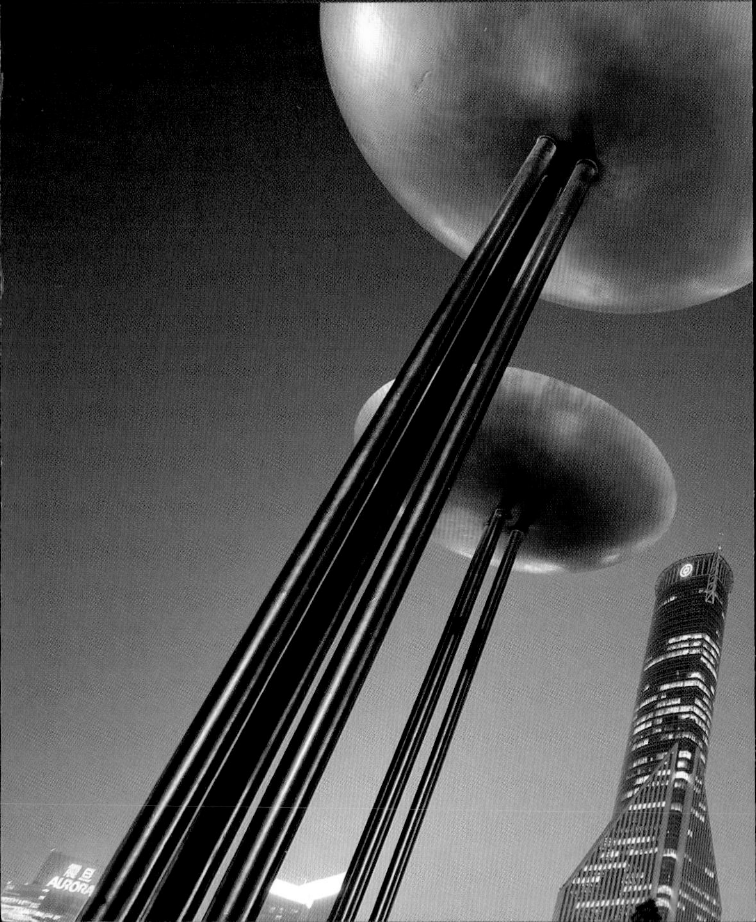

>1	Barrel down the Bund	10
>2	Breeze around People's Square	12
>3	Size up Lujiazui	14
>4	Savour Shanghai's dishy deco heritage	15
>5	Put Frenchtown in the frame	16
>6	Fish for fashion around Tianzifang	18
>7	Drink and dine among Shanghai's *shikumen*	19
>8	Link up with Shanghai's laid-back lanes	20
>9	Rendezvous with art	21
>10	Go on an Old Town culture quest	22
>11	Escape to yesteryear	23
>12	Delve into the divine	24

The illuminated night sky of Pudong (p92)

>1 THE BUND 外滩

BARREL DOWN THE BUND

Beijing has the Great Wall and Xi'an the Terracotta Army, but Shanghai has its Bund, a magnificent riverside sweep of masonry that grew with the rise of Shanghai and impassively watched the city's decline and renaissance. Glittering over the Huangpu River towers is Lujiazui (p14), the Bund's alter ego, which is captured digitally every instant on a cavalcade of cameras. Nowhere else in Shanghai are the ebbing symbols of Western hegemony so deftly contrasted to monuments to China's growing clout.

Originally a muddy towpath, the name Bund (pronounced 'bunned'; more officially 'East Zhongshan No 1 Rd') is an Anglo-Indian word for an embankment. It was to this once-grubby riverside perch that the foreign banks and trading houses brought their ambitious concession-era visions. The spectacle is divided distinctly into the noble procession of neoclassical and art-deco buildings that span from the former British consulate in the north to the McBain Building to the south.

Since the late 1990s, when the penny finally dropped that the Bund's real-estate value was serious cash in the attic, a clutch of august buildings, neglected and mummified during the Cultural Revolution, had their exclusive potential rediscovered and leased out to high-profile tenants. Painfully chic restaurants and bars now jostle for terrace views of Pudong while five-star hotels zero in on remaining parcels of land. The latest big renovations diverted most traffic underground, making the area much more pedestrian friendly.

SLOGANEERING IN SHANGHAI

Stand on the west flank of Waibaidu Bridge and examine the southern river wall on the west side of the bridge. You should see a series of large, partially rubbed out Chinese characters, not far from the bridge. This erstwhile political slogan (*zhengzi kouhao*; Map pp40–1, G1) affords a glimpse into Shanghai's red, revolutionary past. Like the rest of China, and more so, Shanghai has assiduously buried the upheavals of the 1960s and '70s, but such vestiges remain part of the city's political and social heritage. Being partially wiped out, this particular slogan is not entirely legible, but it clearly addresses the spirit of class struggle.

See p51 for a walking tour of the Bund's standout buildings. The promenade is ideal for putting every Bund building in its proper context; it's a carnival of kiosks, hawkers, tour groups and the commercial mayhem of China's tourist boom. Visit at dawn for taichi performers or at dusk to see twilight settle magically over Pudong.

Boat journeys along the Huangpu River (p42) afford first-rate panoramas of the Bund. For a more dignified appreciation of the local charms, dine at one of the choice restaurants (p46), where the setting fully works its magic.

>2 SHANGHAI MUSEUM & PEOPLE'S SQUARE

上海博物馆、人民广场

BREEZE AROUND PEOPLE'S SQUARE

Far less austere than Beijing's crypto-Stalinist Tiananmen Square, People's Square has none of the paranoia of the capital's notorious rectangle. But even if you're twitchy with crowds, you'll find the square is unavoidable due to its combination of a gargantuan metro interchange, intriguing museums, dazzling hotels, top vistas and cultural venues. Ringed by some of Shanghai's most towering skyscrapers at the city's bullseye, People's Square's first stop is undoubtedly the Shanghai Museum (p43). Like an invigorating shot of adrenalin into the leaden legs of Chinese museum-goers, this museum houses a stupefying collection of the cream of Chinese millennia under one roof. It was the first to catapult China's jaded exhibition-goers into the modern age and remains the MagLev of China's museums.

A circular building (designed to replicate a *ding,* an ancient Chinese bronze vessel) at Shanghai's hub, the museum combines a spectacular collection with a first-rate layout. Exhibits range from the high watermarks of Chinese civilisation, to bronzes, stone carvings, ceramics, paintings, jadeware and calligraphy, as well as Ming and Qing furniture and ethnic costumes. Thorough English captions, a light-filled atrium and well spaced-out exhibits are all arcs on an enticing learning curve. If you only visit one museum in China, make it this one.

Cross Renmin Ave to the Shanghai Urban Planning Exhibition Hall (p44) for a peek at Shanghai's electric urban metamorphosis in miniature. Walk west to admire the outlines of the Shanghai Grand Theatre (p50) before turning up North Huangpi Rd to take a look at the Shanghai Art Museum (p43), with aptly named Tomorrow Square – its clawlike apex pointing at some future zeitgeist – towering over you. From the Shanghai Art Museum, follow the northern fringe of People's Park. Hidden in the trees stands the modern-looking Shanghai Museum of Contemporary Art (p43), well worth a visit.

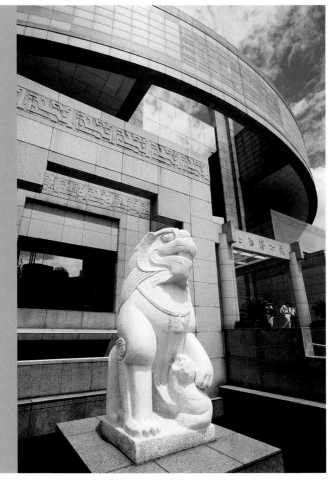

>3 PUDONG 浦东

SIZE UP LUJIAZUI

Nothing in Shanghai is more manufactured and aspirational than Lujiazui, Pudong's most pulsating panorama. The unmistakable steel-and-glass vision would have Mao Zedong choking on his rice porridge and calling for the head of the city mayor. But as Shanghai obsessively compares itself to Hong Kong, the Lujiazui skyline comes as its state-of-the-art answer to Hong Kong's Central district, as viewed from Kowloon. China's economic nerve centre, Lujiazui is an ever-evolving scene. The best way to reflect on China's landmark towers – the colossal Shanghai World Financial Center (p94), the scintillating Jinmao Tower (p94) and the gawky Oriental Pearl TV Tower (p94) – is at night, but any time will do. Weather permitting, toast the towers from the terrace of New Heights (p50) in the Bund. Alternatively, savour high-altitude views – stratocirrus permitting – in Lujiazui itself from Cloud 9 (p97) or the world's highest observation deck in the World Financial Center. And don't forget Pudong's basement attractions: the Shanghai History Museum (p94) and the AP Xinyang Fashion & Gifts Market (p96).

>4 ART DECO SHANGHAI

SAVOUR SHANGHAI'S DISHY DECO HERITAGE

Shanghai is simply a snappy museum of art-deco style. The machine-age building form evokes racy 1920s and '30s Shanghai, when the city first emerged as a modern, cosmopolitan city. The clothing and fashions of that era may have vanished, but art-deco hotels, apartment blocks, private residences, cinemas and banks – made of more durable materials – have survived. Shanghai's masterpiece art-deco relic is the magnificent Peace Hotel (p42). As well as the Broadway Mansions (p51), other survivors in the Bund area include the Bank of China Building (p39), which is a mishmash of styles with a definite deco influence, and the complementary Metropole Hotel and Hamilton House (p68). Farther back near the old racetrack (now People's Square) stands the magnificent Park Hotel (p68), once the tallest building in Asia and which IM Pei claims as an early inspiration, and the nearby Grand Cinema (p68). Both buildings were designed by the legendary architect László Hudec, a Hungarian who was imprisoned in Siberia and escaped to China in 1916. Other notable art-deco buildings include the Cathay Theatre (p68) in the French Concession, the gigantesque abattoir 1933 (p68) across from Factory (p108) and the Paramount Ballroom (p90).

>5 FRENCH CONCESSION 法租界

PUT FRENCHTOWN IN THE FRAME

Put the modish French Concession into focus with a meander around its leafy back streets. From politics to shopping and old gangster pads to gastronomy, entertainment is guaranteed. Starting at spic-and-span Xintiandi (p19) drop by Sun Yatsen's former residence (p66) via pleasant Fuxing Park (p63). The house served as both a Kuomintang base (under Sun) and Communist stronghold (under Song Qingling, his wife). To the north is St Nicholas Church (p66). Dating from 1934, the Russian church has an eccentric CV, spanning shrine, washing-machine factory and French restaurant. Farther along are the 1920s twin villas and garden that now house gallery ShanghART (p63). Point your camera at nearby art-deco masterpieces, such as the Cathay Theatre (p68) and the Jinjiang Hotel (p68). For local fashion, wander Changle Rd and Xinle Rd for their trendy boutiques. One of Shanghai's more eccentric creations is the quirky Moller House (below). Drop by Boonna Café (p79) and thread your way to the Chinese Printed Blue Nankeen Exhibition Hall (p77). The standout sight at the Shanghai Museum of Arts & Crafts (p75) is surely the building. Cap the experience off with dinner and drinks at one of the area's excellent restaurants and bars – Lost Heaven (p79), Baoluo Jiulou (p78), Pinchuan (p79) or Little Face (p80).

MOLLER HOUSE

Shanghai has its European eccentricity, but little prepares you for the Gothic towers and Scandinavian whimsy of the **Moller House** (马勒别墅; 30 S Shaanxi Rd; 陕西南路30号). Built by Eric Moller (the Swedish owner of the Moller Line) and now a hotel, the house was also home to the Communist Youth League. Legend attests that a psychic warned Moller of a tragic end when the house was finished, so the tycoon extended construction time (until 1949). Moller, however, died in a plane crash in 1954.

>6 TAIKANG ROAD ART CENTRE & TIANZIFANG 泰康路艺术中心、田子坊

FISH FOR FASHION AROUND TIANZIFANG

Shoppers and wanderers take note: this engaging warren of *shikumen* (石库门; 'stone-gate houses', see p120) architecture and hip boutiques is the perfect spot for browsing while soaking in the flavours of the ever-elusive traditional Shanghai neighbourhood. The handsome recipe of lane housing, wi-fi cafes, art galleries and fashion shops maximise its presentation, and a living, breathing community still resides here, helping to concoct just the right mood.

Also known as Tianzifang (田子坊), the area consists of three main north–south lanes (Nos 210, 248, 274) criss-crossed by irregular east–west alleyways, which makes exploration slightly disorienting and fun. There are a handful of small galleries and design studios hidden in the old homes and buildings – exhibits can range from photos and posters of old Shanghai to themed collections from global designers. It's tempting to stop immediately at one of the numerous cafes, but spend too much time lounging and you might never find that yak-wool scarf you've always dreamed of. The real activity here is shopping, and the recent explosion of creative start-ups makes for some interesting discoveries, from hand-wrapped pu-erh teas and ethnic embroidery to folk art and retro communist dinnerware. Also explore Courtyard No 7, squeezed to splitting point, and dig among the tangle of alleys filling lanes 248 and 274, which wind past small *shikumen* coffee houses and tucked-away restaurants.

>7 XINTIANDI 新天地

DRINK AND DINE AMONG SHANGHAI'S SHIKUMEN

Xintiandi (see also p66) hasn't even been around for a decade yet and already it's a Shanghai icon. An upscale entertainment complex modelled on traditional *lilong* (alleyway) homes, Xintiandi was the first development in the city to prove that historic architecture does, in fact, have economic value. Elsewhere that might sound like a no-brainer, but in 21st-century China, which is head-over-heels for the bulldozer, it came as quite a revelation. Well-heeled shoppers and alfresco diners keep the place busy until late, and if you're looking for a memorable meal or a browse through some of Shanghai's more fashionable shops, this is the place.

The heart of the complex, divided into a pedestrianised north and south block, consists of largely rebuilt traditional *shikumen* houses, brought bang up-to-date with a stylish modern spin. But while the layout suggests a flavour of yesteryear, you shouldn't expect much in the cultural realm. Xintiandi doesn't deliver any of the lived-in charm of the Taikang Road Art Centre (opposite) or the creaking, rickety simplicity of the Old Town. Beyond two worthwhile sights – the Shikumen Open House Museum (p63) and the Site of the 1st National Congress of the CCP (p63) – it's best for shopping, strolling the prettified alleyways and enjoying a summer's evening over drinks or a meal. Pick up an orientation map at the Shanghai Information Centre for International Visitors (p152) on Xingye Rd.

>8 LONGTANG & LILONG

LINK UP WITH SHANGHAI'S LAID-BACK LANES

Shanghai's zappy, ultramodern skyline is electric for sure, but also impersonal and dwarfing. Don't fret. For things on a more human scale, where real communities get on with their daily lives, meandering through Shanghai's collection of *lilong* alleys (里弄; also known as *longtang*, 弄堂) and *shikumen* homes is a helpful antidote. These gorgeous stone-and-brick communities, mainly designed from the mid-19th century to the art-deco era, hog much of Shanghai's characteristic Concession-era charms, where low-rise tenements line up in neat, pretty rows.

Visitors tend to get their first *shikumen* preamble at slick Xintiandi (p66), though Taikang Road Art Centre (p66) is a more intimate proposition. Also wander along Yuyuan Rd (愚园路) in Jing'an; some of Shanghai's most picturesque *lilong* alleys are invitingly tucked away from its tree-shaded length. Delve down Bubbling Well Lane or 611 Yuyuan Rd and hunt down the Bubbling Well Road Apartments (p90). Whether you're walking down Huaihai Rd or North Jiangxi Rd, look out for portals leading down busy, and at times decrepit, alleyways, typically identified by the last character *fang* (坊) or *li* (里).

>9 M50 莫干山路50号

RENDEZVOUS WITH ART

Shanghai's spot-on answer to Beijing's larger 798 Art District, M50 (50 Moganshan Rd, p83) is one of the few parts of town you get to see graffiti. Its utilitarian industrial buildings – warehouse-sized with big, bright windows – largely date to the 1930s and 1940s: ideal for displaying art, while supplying the obligatory proletarian frisson which fires up so much of modern Chinese art.

Like all of Shanghai's galleries, cutting-edge work is sometimes surrounded by mediocrity, so prepare to sift and do your homework if you're in a buying frame of mind. Standout galleries include the huge display spaces of ShanghART, Art Scene and island6. The latter focuses on collaborative works created in a studio behind the gallery. Bandu Cabin (p90) serves noodles, peanut butter sandwiches and coffee while Shirt Flag (p67) and other trendy stores snare shopaholics. Most galleries are open 10am to 7pm, but many shut on Monday.

>10 YUYUAN GARDENS & BAZAAR
豫园、豫园商城

GO ON AN OLD TOWN CULTURE QUEST

With its shaded alcoves, sparkling pools flashing with goldfish, beckoning classical pavilions, rustling bamboo and rocky recesses, Yuyuan Gardens (p58) is one of Shanghai's most eminent sights. This prompts a caveat: classical Chinese gardens were simply not designed to accommodate daily visitor figures topping a thousand. Securing that unique, tranquil atmosphere that brought these gardens fame can be a mission improbable. Set your alarm for an early, precrowd visit for glimpses of the gardens' tranquilising harmonies of light and shade, and rock and water. Weekends are strictly for those who like their tourists wall-to-wall or for impressions of Shanghai's world-beating urban densities.

The larger, adjacent Yuyuan Bazaar (p59) is similarly overrun, but the pandemonium is quite in keeping with its full-on commercial mayhem.

>11 CLASSICAL CHINA

ESCAPE TO YESTERYEAR

When you tire of Shanghai's slick, international modernity, head for the quintessentially Chinese landscapes out of town. The Yangzi Delta area, traditionally known as the land of fish and rice, has long been one of the most prosperous parts of the Middle Kingdom. The big centres of trade in dynastic times were Hangzhou (p110), capital of the empire from AD 1127 to 1276, and Suzhou (p112), the southern terminus of the 7th-century Grand Canal, the main link between north and south China for centuries. Today these two cities, with their remnants of affluence and cultural sophistication, are among the most popular destinations in the country. Hangzhou's West Lake and tea plantations inspire tranquil bike rides; the gardens of Suzhou enthral art aficionados. Strewn across the rest of the delta are picturesque whitewashed canal towns with cobbled lanes, humpbacked bridges and original Ming and Qing architecture. Watch out for garishly made-over places such as Zhouzhuang (the 'number-one canal town') and try to get to less-crowded villages such as Zhujiajiao (p114) and Tongli (p115). Qibao (p100) doesn't quite match the allure of the latter, but if you're short on time, it's only a hop, skip and metro ride away, making it a much more practical option for a short trip from Shanghai.

>12 JADE BUDDHA TEMPLE 玉佛寺

DELVE INTO THE DIVINE

Here, the tinkle of the tourist dollar jars with the sacred chanting of monks and birds chirping from *Magnolia grandiflora* branches, but this remains Shanghai's holiest Buddhist shrine. Festooned with red lanterns, the halls and courtyards of the saffron-coloured temple (p83) glitter with fine effigies and temple ornaments. A visit is a reminder of the growing religious fever sweeping China. Admire the extravagant statue of Weituo in the Hall of Heavenly Kings, displayed back-to-back with Milefo in a fabulous case with glass panes. The highlight is the namesake 1.9m-tall Jade Buddha *(Yufo)*. Exhibited in a carved wooden cabinet, the pale-green, cool effigy of Sakyamuni from Myanmar is unapproachable, but you can gaze at it from the far side of a wooden barrier. The similarly styled Reclining Buddha *(Wofo)*, a smiling, white-jade figure, head propped up on one palm and the other arm lying femininely on his side, lies downstairs. Opposite is a much larger and less artful modern copy in stone. The main hall, the Great Treasure Hall, is dedicated to the worship of the past, present and future Buddhas, flanked by towering gilded *luohan* (arhat). If the vegie munchies hit, the temple has a popular vegetarian restaurant attached. If you can, get here during the Chinese New Year (p26).

>SHANGHAI DIARY

Whenever you travel to Shanghai, your trip may coincide with local festivities and holidays. This can be a colourful and entertaining time to be in town, especially when events you can participate in take place. Major traditional Chinese festivals are calculated according to the lunar calendar. Western festivals are making big inroads and even Valentine's Day has become a date on the romantic calendar. Christmas is a major commercial milestone at the end of the year, perhaps unsurprisingly for a city at the apex of China's consumer boom.

The Lantern Festival (p26) lights up the city

JANUARY TO FEBRUARY

Western New Year 元旦

Celebrated in wild style in bars citywide, the New Year also sees celebrations – including lion and dragon dances – at the Longhua Temple (p100).

Chinese New Year 春节

Also called the Spring Festival, this is the Chinese equivalent of Christmas. Families get together to feast on dumplings, exchange gifts, vegetate in front of the TV, visit friends and take a long holiday. The festival traditionally commences on the first day of the lunar calendar (3 February 2011; 23 January 2012). At the stroke of midnight, a huge cavalcade of fireworks welcomes the New Year and wards off bad spirits. Families paste red couplets on their doors and hand out *hongbao,* red envelopes stuffed with money. The high point of the lunar calendar, it's followed by a week's holiday. This is a bad time to be on the road – airfares soar, trains are packed with migrant workers returning home and hotels are booked solid.

Valentine's Day 情人节

The traditional Chinese festival for lovers – held on the seventh day of the seventh lunar month (七夕) – has been usurped by the Western celebration. Valentine's Day (14 February) is taken seriously by Shanghai suitors as an occasion for a massive blow-out.

Lantern Festival 元宵节

This festival, on the 15th day of the first lunar month (17 February 2011; 6 February 2012), is celebrated by eating *yuanxiao* or *tangyuan* (dumplings of glutinous rice with sweet fillings) and hanging lanterns. Festivities also occur in the Yuyuan Gardens (p58).

MARCH TO MAY

Shanghai International Literary Festival
上海国际文学艺术节

Book lovers, literati and cognoscenti descend on the Glamour Bar (p50; tickets cost Y65, including one drink) in March/April for the city's top literary event, attended by both international and local authors.

Birthday of Guanyin
观世音生日

The Buddhist Goddess of Mercy has her birthday on the 19th day of the second moon (2 April 2010; 22 March 2011; 10 March 2012), an excellent time to visit Buddhist temples.

Qingming Festival 清明节

Also called the Tomb-Sweeping Festival, Shanghainese visit and clean the graves of their dearly departed on 5 April (4 April in leap years) and worship their ancestors.

Longhua Temple Fair
龙华寺庙会

Often commencing in April (16 April 2010; 5 April 2011; 24 March 2012) and held over several weeks into May, this temple fair begins on the third day of the third lunar month and there are stalls, jugglers and stilt walkers.

Formula 1
www.formula1.com

The slick Shanghai International Circuit hosts several high-profile motor-racing competitions, including the hotly contested F1 (Y380 to Y3980) in April (dates subject to change).

JUNE

Dragon Boat Festival 端午节

Celebrated on the fifth day of the fifth lunar month (16 June 2010; 6 June 2011; 23 June 2012), dragon boats are raced along the Huangpu River in honour of the death of 3rd-century-BC poet-statesman Qu Yuan.

Shanghai International Film Festival 上海国际电影节
www.siff.com

With screenings at various cinemas around Shanghai, the movie-going festival brings international and locally produced films to town. It's most popular with locals; reserve tickets for the most high-profile films.

JULY TO SEPTEMBER

Mid-Autumn Festival 中秋节

Also called the Moon Festival, Chinese celebrate by sharing delicious moon cakes, gazing

at the moon and having a get-together. The festival is held on the 15th day of the eighth lunar month (22 September 2010; 12 September 2011; 30 September 2012).

Shanghai Biennale 上海双年展
www.shanghaibiennale.org

Staged once every two years, this popular international arts festival is held at the Shanghai Art Museum (p43). It's to be held from September to November in 2010.

OCTOBER TO NOVEMBER

National Day 国庆节

Held on 1 October but often morphing into a week-long holiday, Shanghai Chinese take their hard-earned cash and hit the road, inundating tourist sites and putting the transport network under severe strain.

Halloween 万圣节

Another foreign import, latched onto for its ghouls and goblins, pagan All Hallows' Eve is increasingly popular among young Shanghainese. Check the expat magazines for details of costume parties in bars around town. Don't expect trick-or-treating, though.

Masters Cup 网球大师杯
www.masters-cup.com

Shanghai's premier tennis tournament is staged at the Qi Zhong Stadium in October or November.

Acrobatics at the Shanghai Centre Theatre (p91)

China Shanghai International Arts Festival
中国上海国际艺术节

www.artsbird.com

A month-long program of cultural events held in October and November, including the Shanghai Art Fair, international music, dance, opera, acrobatics and the Shanghai Biennale (p27).

Shanghai International Marathon 上海国际马拉松赛

www.shmarathon.com

Starting on the Bund, the annual late-November trot through the streets of Shanghai attracts around 12,000 runners. Other events include a half-marathon and a 4.5km 'health race'.

DECEMBER

Christmas Day 圣诞节

Santa Claus doesn't need a visa to hand out presents citywide to starry-eyed kids as Christmas drags its huge, articulated commercial bonanza into town. Services are held in Shanghai's many churches (p134).

Taichi on the Bund promenade (p38)

ITINERARIES

With so many facets and angles for exploration, Shanghai can seem a daunting destination. To help time-manage your trip and get the most from Shanghai, the following itineraries will give you suggestions for maximising your stay. If you are here for long enough, earmark trips to Hangzhou (p110) and Zhujiajiao (p114).

ONE DAY

Rise with the sun for early-morning riverside scenes on the Bund (p10) as the vast city stirs from its slumber. Come round with a coffee at Bund 12 Café (p49) before strolling along East Nanjing Rd to People's Square and the Shanghai Museum (p12), or, depending on your mindset, the Shanghai Urban Planning Exhibition Hall (p44). After lunch at Yang's Fry Dumplings (p48), hop on the metro at People's Square to shuttle east to Pudong. Explore the fun and interactive Shanghai History Museum (p94) or contemplate the Bund from the breezy Riverside Promenade (p94) and then take a highspeed lift to the world's highest observation deck, inside the World Financial Center (p94), to put Shanghai in perspective. Ferry back across the river and have a table booked for dinner at Tiandi (p48) or Xindalu (p108), followed by a nightcap at the Glamour Bar (p50) or New Heights (p50).

TWO DAYS

Pre-empt the crowds with an early start at the Old Town's Yuyuan Gardens before poking around for souvenirs at Old Street (p58) and wandering the alleyways. Make your next stop Xintiandi (p19) for lunch and a visit to the Shikumen Open House Museum (p63). Taxi it to Taikang Road Art Centre (p18) for the afternoon. Further explore the French Concession before dining at Di Shui Dong (p69). Caught a second wind? Catch the acrobats (p81), go clubbing at Sin Lounge (p91) or unwind with a traditional Chinese massage (p128).

THREE DAYS

Continue where you left off, roaming the French Concession, before exploring the maze of galleries at M50 (p21) via the Jade Buddha Temple

Top left Shoes and fashion at the Taikang Road Art Centre (p18) **Top right** Coffee at Xintiandi (p19) **Bottom** Street stalls in Hongkou (p104)

ITINERARIES

(p24). Fish for pearls and haggle for bargains at the Fenshine Fashion &
Accessories Plaza (p86) before taking in a meal at Fu 1039 (p87). Alternatively, take the day off and escape to the canal towns of Zhujiajiao (p114)
or Tongli (p115).

RAINY SHANGHAI

Spend the day in the Shanghai Museum (p12) and then sprint with your
umbrella from sight to sight in People's Square taking in the Shanghai Urban Planning Exhibition Hall (p44), the Shanghai Museum of Contemporary Art (p43) and the Shanghai Art Museum (p43). Hop from art gallery
to art gallery at M50 (p21) and browse the traditional music collection at
Bandu Cabin (p90). Hide away in the Shanghai History Museum (p94) or
sneak into a burlesque show at Chinatown (p108).

SHOPPING SHANGHAI

Come to Shanghai specifically to shop? For local fashion, the first stop
should be the French Concession East district. The Taikang Road Art
Centre is the most fun, with outlets of many of the city's most unique
stores. For swish local brands such as Annabel Lee (p44), be sure to stop
by Xintiandi. To get more off the beaten track, head to the boutique
streets of Changle Rd and Xinle Rd (p126), where local designers such as
La Vie are located. Tailored clothing is a speciality of Shanghai – for silk
and cashmere clothing made to order, stop by the Shiliupu Fabric Market

FORWARD PLANNING

Three weeks before you go Leaf through some good Shanghai-related reading (p141) and
sit through a film or two on Shanghai (p142). Check some of Shanghai's top websites (p147)
and find out the latest from local media (p150). Check to see if your trip coincides with popular festivals or clashes with the big Chinese holiday periods (p25). Make sure your passport
and visa are in order (p143). Check your vaccinations are up to date, invest in a phrasebook
and make a start learning some Mandarin.

Two weeks before you go Give some thought to possible itineraries and how to best plan
your time, especially if you are planning some trips out of town (p109). Scout around for good
hotel deals (p118) and reserve a room. A very wise move would be to book a table at one of
Shanghai's standout restaurants, such as T8 (p70).

The day before you leave Check your flight (and water the indoor plants and check the
locks).

(p59); for Chinese-style dresses and jackets, try stores such as Heping Finery (p67) on South Maoming Rd. Bargain hunting also rates high on shoppers' to-do lists: the Fenshine Fashion & Accessories Plaza (p86) has three floors of quality clothing and pearls, but for sheer size, nothing beats the AP Xinyang Fashion & Gifts Market (p96) in Pudong. Locals love the Qipu Market (p107), which has the lowest prices in the city – just don't expect brand names. Looking for handicrafts, funky ceramics or herbal beauty supplies? Head to the French Concession West district (p75)…but we'll stop here!

FOR FREE

So, have you overextended the credit card yet? No worries, there are enough freebies in Shanghai to keep you occupied. Near the Bund are the Post Museum (p107) and the Metersbonwe Costume Museum (p42); both are excellent. The standout Shanghai Museum (p12) is gratis, as are the numerous art galleries at M50 (p21) and those scattered throughout the French Concession (see the boxed text, p66). Strolling the French Concession or the Bund (p51) doesn't cost a cent. Further out in Xujia-hui, catch up on China's little-known seafaring history at the CY Tung Maritime Museum (p74) or reserve a spot on a Saturday tour of the Jesuit Bibliotheca Zi-Ka-Wei (p100).

>NEIGHBOURHOODS

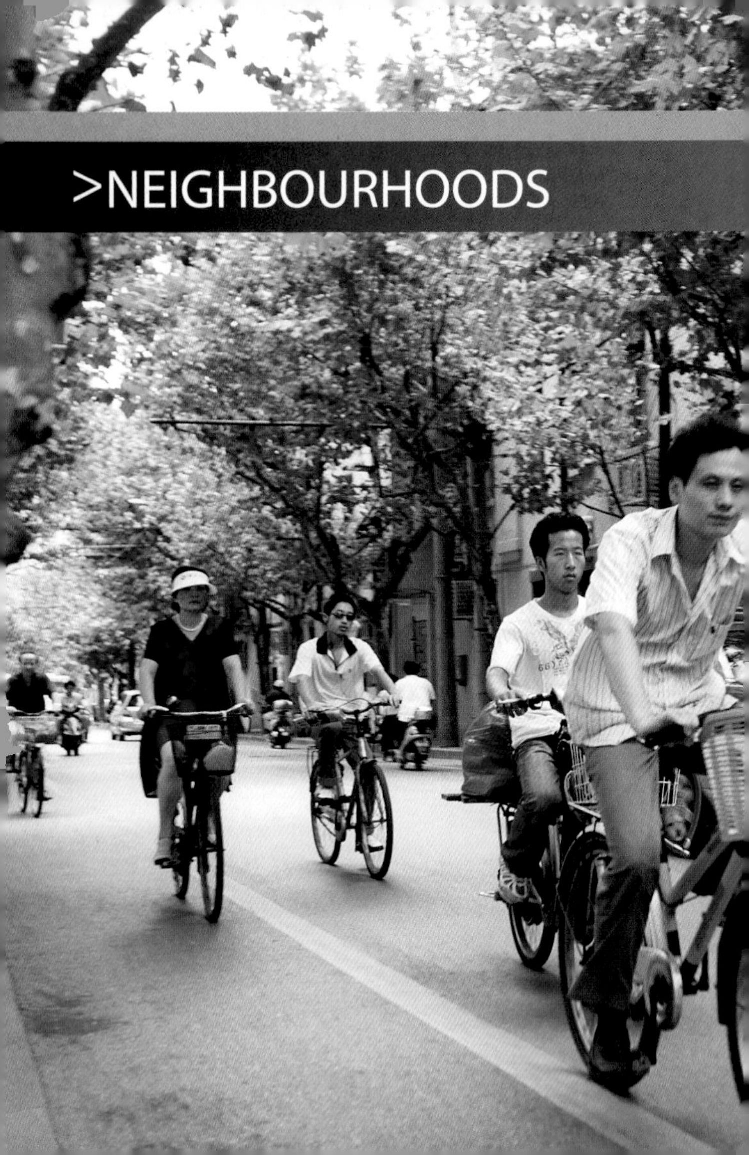

>1 The Bund & People's Square 38
>2 Old Town 54
>3 French Concession East 62
>4 French Concession West 72
>5 Jing'an 82
>6 Pudong 92
>7 Xujiahui & South Shanghai 98
>8 Hongkou & North Shanghai 104

Cycling in the French Concession (p62)

NEIGHBOURHOODS

Slashed by the winding brown waters of the Huangpu River, Shanghai conveniently cleaves into two distinct entities: Puxi (浦西) to the west and Pudong (浦东) to the east.

Shanghai is a tale of two cities. The enticing Shanghai of yesteryear – its grand architecture, delightful side streets and charismatic historic narrative – belongs exclusively to Puxi. Sky-scraping Pudong serves as a brash steel-and-concrete symbol of Shanghai's towering economic stature. Lashed together by vast bridges, Puxi and Pudong are almost two different nation states, their only common ground a shared glut of five-star hotels.

Fragmented into a rambling jigsaw of districts and neighbourhoods, Puxi's divisions largely echo the integrity of the former Concession layout. Knee-deep in history, the Bund and East Nanjing Rd is Shanghai's most iconic locale, a wham-bam confluence of grand buildings, landmark architecture, ambitious restaurants, glamorous bars and commercial verve. On the district's western fringe – as East Nanjing Rd finally runs out of commercial puff – busy People's Square is the geographic focus of town, overlooked by a growing forest of sci-fi-inspired skyscrapers.

The dishevelled Old Town south of the Bund is Shanghai's original settlement, where traces of pre-Concession history lock horns with developers. South of here is the recently developed World Expo site.

Expect to be shanghaied by the city's most elegant district, the French Concession, a delightful concoction of leafy backstreets, *shikumen* (stone-gate houses), gorgeous *lilong* (alleyways), 1930s villas, art-deco architecture, trendy boutiques and up-to-the-minute restaurants, bars and shops.

Powering north of the French Concession is the vibrant commercial district of Jing'an, anchored to bustling West Nanjing Rd, with its abundance of period architecture, malls, top-end hotels and charming *lilong* architecture.

Xujiahui and South Shanghai stand out for their landmark Jesuit artefacts, while the up-and-coming district of Hongkou and North Shanghai sprawls north of the Bund.

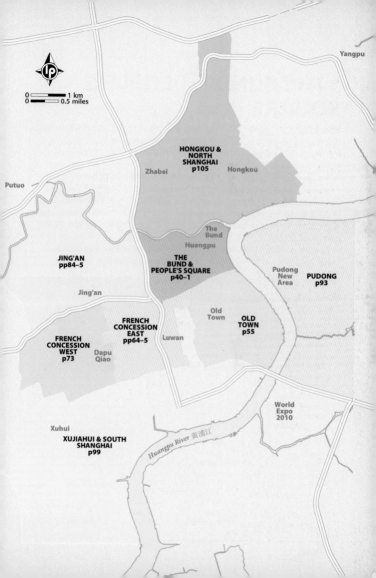

>THE BUND & PEOPLE'S SQUARE

The Bund is Shanghai's stately sweep of prestigious architecture, top-flight restaurants, exclusive shopping and iconic views. Wisely transformed into a pedestrian area in 2009, the promenade is the first stop for all visitors to Shanghai. Pudong's steel skyline glitters eastwards, reflecting China's new era, but Shanghai as a historic phenomenon – its inimitable biography, its hybrid allegiances of East and West, its decades of excess – was shaped here. The Bund evokes the city's cosmopolitan and decadent heyday like no other. The roads immediately west form a gritty district of Concession-era buildings, where a tatty grandeur reigns.

Breezing west all the way from the art-deco masterpiece Peace Hotel (p42) to Shanghai's focal point, People's Square, is East Nan-

THE BUND & PEOPLE'S SQUARE

◉ SEE

Bank of China	1	G2
Bund History Museum	2	H1
Bund Museum	3	H3
Contrasts Art Gallery	4	G3
Customs House	5	G2
Hongkong & Shanghai Banking Corporation (HSBC) building	6	G3
Huangpu Park	7	G1
Huangpu River Cruise	8	H4
Metersbonwe Costume Museum	9	F2
Peace Hotel	10	G2
Shanghai Art Museum	11	C4
Shanghai Gallery of Art	(see 19)	
Shanghai Museum	12	D5
Shanghai Museum of Contemporary Art (MOCA Shanghai)	13	C4
Shanghai Urban Planning Exhibition Hall	14	D4

⌂ SHOP

Annabel Lee	(see 17)	
Blue Shanghai White	15	G3
Shanghai Museum Art Store	(see 12)	
Shanghai No 1 (First) Food Store	16	D3
Shiatzy Chen	17	G3
Suzhou Cobblers	(see 15)	
Yunhong Chopsticks Shop	(see 9)	

⑪ EAT

Ajisen	(see 22)	
Gongdelin	18	B4
Jean Georges	19	H3
M on the Bund	20	G3
Shanghai Grandmother	21	G3
South Memory	22	F2
Tiandi	23	G3
Wuyue Renjia	24	E3

Yang's Fry Dumplings	25	C3
Yunnan Rd Food Street	26	E5

▼ DRINK

Bar Rouge	27	G2
Barbarossa	28	C4
Bund 12 Café	(see 6)	
Captain's Bar	29	G3
Glamour Bar	(see 20)	
New Heights	(see 19)	

★ PLAY

Cabaret	(see 23)	
M1NT	30	F3
Shanghai Concert Hall	31	D5
Shanghai Grand Theatre	32	C4
Yifu Theatre	33	D4

Please see over for map

jing Rd, China's most famous shopping drag. You won't find Shanghai's standout boutiques here, but it's perennially thick with eager shoppers, out-of-towners and neon signs illuminating the night. Take a deep breath, plunge in, but shrug off English-speaking girls (see the boxed text, p43) dragging foreigners to overpriced cafes.

◉ SEE

◉ BANK OF CHINA BUILDING
中国银行

23 E Zhongshan No 1 Rd; 中山东一路 **23** 号; Ⓜ **E Nanjing Rd**

A glorious meld of Chinese and Western architectural styling, this 1937 building is a neat collusion of deco and Middle Kingdom motifs. Check out the funky modern-style Chinese lions out the front.

◉ BUND MUSEUM 外滩博物馆

1 E Zhongshan No 2 Rd; 中山东二路 **1** 号; **admission free;** 🕑 **9am-5pm;** Ⓜ **E Nanjing Rd**

The 'museum' runs to little more than a smattering of photos, but explore the building housing it, the Meteorological Signal Tower (外滩信号台), erected by industrious Jesuits.

◉ CONTRASTS 对比窗艺廊

☎ **6323 1989; 181 Middle Jiangxi Rd;** 江西中路**181**号; 🕑 **10am-10pm** Ⓜ **E Nanjing Rd**

This art gallery is most notable for its owner – Hong Kong property heiress and socialite Pearl Lam – who has a string of galleries around the world and is an influential figure in China's contemporary art scene.

◉ CUSTOMS HOUSE

13 E Zhongshan No 1 Rd; 中山东一路 **13** 号; Ⓜ **E Nanjing Rd**

The magnificent Customs House dates from 1925, capped with a clock face and 'Big Ching', a bell substituted during the Cultural Revolution with loudspeakers broadcasting revolutionary songs.

Revolutionary relief at Customs House

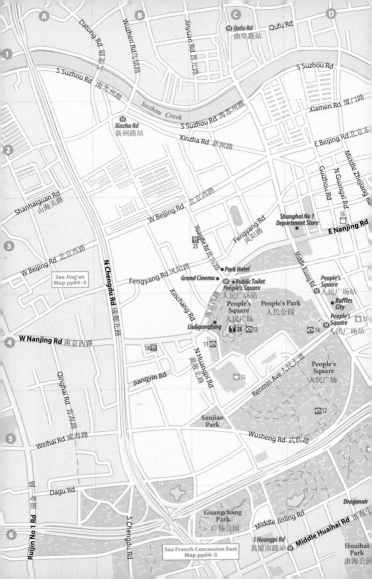

Map Grid References

A
B
C
D

1
2
3
4
5
6

Datong Rd 大通路
Wuzhen Rd 乌镇路
Jinyuan Rd 晋元路
Qufu Rd 曲阜路站
Qufu Rd

S Suzhou Rd 南苏州路
S Suzhou Rd
S Suzhou Rd 南苏州路

Suzhou Creek

Xiamen Rd 厦门路
E Beijing Rd 北京东
Middle Zhejiang Rd
N Guangxi Rd
Guizhou Rd

Xinzha Rd
新闸路站
Xinzha Rd 新闸路

Shanhaiguan Rd
山海关路

W Beijing Rd
北京西路
Fengyang Rd 凤阳路

Shanghai No 1
Department Store
E Nanjing Rd
16

W Beijing Rd 北京西路
N Chengdu Rd 成都北路

See Jing'an
Map pp84–5

Park Hotel
Fengyang Rd 凤阳路
25
Huangpi Rd N 黄陂北路
People's
Square 人民广场站

Grand Cinema ●
Public Toilet
People's Square
人民广场站

People's
Square
Raffles
City
People's
Square
人民广场站

Xinchang Rd 新昌路

People's
Square
人民广场
People's Park
人民公园

W Nanjing Rd 南京西路

Liuligongfang

28 13

18 17
11

14

Jiangyin Rd
N Huangpi Rd 黄陂北路

32

Renmin Ave 人民大道

People's
Square
人民广场

Qinghai Rd 青海路

Sanjiao
Park

12

Weihai Rd 威海路

Wusheng Rd 武胜路

Dagu Rd

Ruijin No 1 Rd

S Chengdu Rd 成都南路

Guangchang
Park
广场公园
Middle Jinling Rd

Dragonair

Middle Huaihai Rd 淮海中路

S Huangpi Rd
黄陂南路站

Huaihai
Park
淮海公园

See French Concession East
Map pp64–5

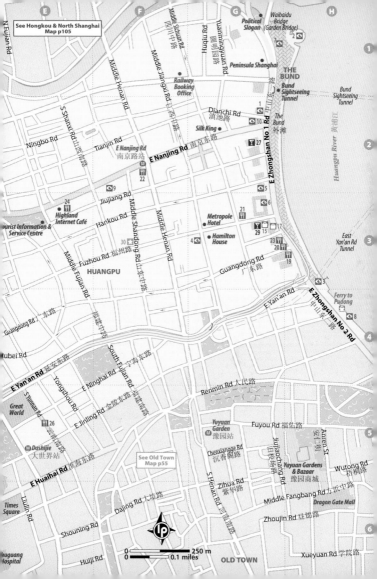

🔘 HONGKONG & SHANGHAI BANKING CORPORATION (HSBC) BUILDING 汇丰银行

12 E Zhongshan No 1 Rd; 中山东一路12号; Ⓜ E Nanjing Rd

Put a crick in your neck gawping at the ceiling mosaic portraying the 12 zodiac signs and the world's eight great banking centres. When it went up in 1923, the domed building was commonly known as 'the finest building east of Suez'.

🔘 HUANGPU PARK 黄浦公园

Ⓜ E Nanjing Rd

China's first ever public park (1868) achieved lasting notoriety for its apocryphal 'No Dogs or Chinese allowed' sign. The park today is blighted by the Monument to the People's Heroes, above the **Bund History Museum** (外滩历史纪念馆; admission free; 🕙 9am-4pm).

🔘 HUANGPU RIVER 黄浦江游览

☎ 6374 4461; 219-239 E Zhongshan No 2 Rd; 中山东二路219-239号; Ⓜ E Nanjing Rd

The Huangpu River offers staggering views of the Bund and riverfront activity. Skip the marathon chug to Wusongkou (Y150, 3½ hours, 2pm) at the Yangzi River mouth for the one-hour trip to Yangpu Bridge (Y50/70 day/night) or the popular 30-minute cruises from the Pearl Dock (Y50/70 day/night) in Lujiazui. Most boats depart from the south end of the Bund, where tickets are sold. Alternatively, take the six-minute **ferry ride** (轮渡; Y2; 🕙 7am-10pm) across the river to Pudong. It leaves from the southern end of the Bund.

🔘 METERSBONWE COSTUME MUSEUM 美特斯邦威服饰博物馆

☎ 6352 7801; 5th fl, 387 E Nanjing Rd; 南京东路387号5楼; admission free; 🕙 10am-10pm; Ⓜ E Nanjing Rd

This captivating private museum was opened by the owner of Chinese fashion giant Metersbonwe to display the traditional attire of Han Chinese and ethnic groups from around the country. The collection is extensive, ranging from Emperor Qianlong's dragon robes and Shanghai *qipao* (cheongsam) to delicate embroidery from China's southwest, and even an outfit made of salmon skin.

🔘 PEACE HOTEL 和平饭店

☎ 6321 6888; www.fairmont.com; 20 E Nanjing Rd; 南京东路20号; Ⓜ E Nanjing Rd

Shanghai's most treasured art-deco monument was built between 1926 and 1929 as the Cathay by Victor Sassoon. Frequented by well-heeled celebrities (from George Bernard Shaw to Noel Coward), the riff-raff slept elsewhere. Renovations (it's now the Fairmont Peace Hotel) will hopefully have restored it to its original splendour.

☉ SHANGHAI ART MUSEUM
上海美术馆
☎ 6327 2829; 325 W Nanjing Rd; 南京西路325号; admission Y20; ☉ 9am-5pm (last entry 4pm); Ⓜ People's Square
Venue of the Shanghai Biennale (p25), this space is attractively housed within the former British Racecourse Club building. The architecture is noteworthy, but the exhibitions can be inconsistent.

☉ SHANGHAI GALLERY OF ART 沪申画廊
☎ 6321 5757; www.threeonthebund .com; 3rd fl, Three on the Bund, 3 E Zhongshan No 1 Rd; 外滩3号3楼; admission free; Ⓜ E Nanjing Rd
This gallery oozes exclusivity and style. Works include photorealist art, photography and conceptual pieces, displayed in a spacious art space.

☉ SHANGHAI MUSEUM
上海博物馆
☎ 6372 3500; 201 Renmin Ave (entrance on E Yan'an Rd); 人民大道201号; admission free; ☉ 9am-5pm (last entry 4pm); Ⓜ People's Square
A tour de force, this museum (see also p12) of traditional Chinese

SCAMS
'Hello, can you help us take photo?' This ostensibly harmless question is in fact one of the better hooks for Shanghai's main scam. Young people posing as students work the main tourist drags – the Bund, East Nanjing Rd and the exit of the Shanghai Museum – engaging tourists in conversation. However the conversation begins, it will inevitably end with an invitation to a 'traditional tea ceremony'. Intrigued? Don't be. You'll wind up with a US$100 bill and a private escort to the closest ATM.

art is the centrepiece of People's Square, if not Shanghai, so bookmark a whole day. Top galleries include the Ceramics Gallery, Bronzes Gallery and Painting Gallery. Arrive early to avoid the queues.

☉ SHANGHAI MUSEUM OF CONTEMPORARY ART (MOCA SHANGHAI) 上海当代艺术馆
☎ 6327 9900; People's Park; 人民公园; admission Y20; ☉ 10am-6pm Thu-Tue, 10am-10pm Wed; Ⓜ People's Square
With its all-glass construction squeezing every last photon from Shanghai's murky sunlight, this independent museum is doing a cracking job of bringing contemporary international artwork to the city.

🖒 SHANGHAI URBAN PLANNING EXHIBITION HALL
上海城市规划展示馆

☎ 6318 4477; 100 Renmin Ave (entrance on Middle Xizang Rd); 人民大道100号; admission Y30; ⏱ 9am-5pm Tue-Thu (last entry 4pm), 9am-6pm Fri-Sun (last entry 5pm), closed Mon; Ⓜ People's Square

Some cities romanticise their past, others promise good times in the present, but only in China are you expected to visit places that haven't even been built yet. The 3rd floor features Shanghai's idealised future, with an incredible model layout of the megalopolis-to-come plus a dizzying Virtual World 3-D wrap-around tour complete with celebratory fireworks.

🛍 SHOP

🖿 ANNABEL LEE 安梨 Fashion

☎ 6445 8218; No 1, Lane 8, E Zhongshan No 1 Rd; 中山东一路8弄1号; ⏱ 10am-10pm; Ⓜ E Nanjing Rd

An elegant shop with a gorgeous range of soft-coloured and playfully designed accessories in silk, linen and cashmere, many of which feature delicate and stylish embroidery.

🖿 BLUE SHANGHAI WHITE
海晨 Ceramics

☎ 6352 2222; Unit 103, 17 Fuzhou Rd; 福州路17号103房; ⏱ 10.30am-6.30pm; Ⓜ E Nanjing Rd

This petite shop has a delightful collection of exquisite hand-painted ceramics, including porcelain tea cups, teapots and vases. Prices start at around Y80 for a small cup and saucer.

🖿 SHANGHAI MUSEUM ART STORE 上海博物馆艺术品商店
Souvenirs, Arts

☎ 6327 4514; 201 Renmin Ave; 人民大道201号; ⏱ 9am-4pm; Ⓜ People's Square

Save energy after seeing the Shanghai Museum (p43) for this emporium. Items include facsimiles of the museum's porcelain collection, and postcards and books on the Chinese arts, architecture, travel and language.

🖿 SHANGHAI NO 1 (FIRST) FOOD STORE 上海市第一食品商店 Food

720 E Nanjing Rd; 南京东路720号; ⏱ 9.30am-10pm; Ⓜ E Nanjing Rd

It's bedlam, but this is how the Shanghainese shop and it's lots of fun. Trawl the ground floor for dried mushrooms, ginseng, moon cakes and dried fruit.

🖿 SHIATZY CHEN 夏姿 Fashion

☎ 6321 9155; 9 East Zhongshan No 1 Rd; 中山东一路9号; ⏱ 10am-10pm; Ⓜ E Nanjing Rd

This fashion store has elegant, uber-exclusive clothing creations

Erica Ding

Erica, 27, is from the northwestern province of Gansu. She moved to Shanghai in 2005 and now works as an assistant trade commissioner for a foreign consulate.

What do you think of the Shanghainese? In the past, the locals were dominant. If you didn't speak their dialect, it was difficult to find work or communicate. But now they accept you. All kinds of people have come here; everyone has brought their own culture to develop a new Shanghai. **Why do you think Shanghai is a good place to do business?** Because this is China's front door. Foreign companies enter the market in Shanghai; it's easier here. **What are your favourite places to eat?** I like to eat Thai, Greek, Middle Eastern and Uighur food. One place I go is the Uighur Restaurant (p70). **If you could change one thing in Shanghai…**No more scooters riding on the footpath!

NEIGHBOURHOODS

THE BUND & PEOPLE'S SQUARE

from the celebrated Taiwanese designer, with swish East-meets-West styles.

👜 SUZHOU COBBLERS 上海起想艺术品 Shoes

☎ 6321 7087; Unit 101, 17 Fuzhou Rd; 福州路17号101室; ⏰ 10.30am-6.30pm; Ⓜ E Nanjing Rd

You may need to shoehorn yourself into this shoebox of a shop space off the Bund. The micro outlet plies dainty, hand-embroidered silk slippers and shoes and has a range of colourful bags, hats and lanterns.

🥢 YUNHONG CHOPSTICKS SHOP 韵泓筷子店 Souvenirs

☎ 6322 0207; 387 E Nanjing Rd; 南京东路387号; ⏰ 9am-10.30pm; Ⓜ E Nanjing Rd

One-stop chopstick shopping is sorted at this busy shop on the East Nanjing Rd drag. Chopsticks range from basic wooden models for so-so friends back home to solid silver sets (the precious metal dispels toxins) for your current crush.

🍴 EAT

The Bund is a prestigious and much-vaunted perch for the cream of Shanghai's exclusive restaurants, which have an international slant.

🍴 GONGDELIN 功德林
Chinese   YYY

☎ 6327 0218; 445 W Nanjing Rd; 南京西路445号; ⏰ 11am-3pm & 5-10.30pm; Ⓜ People's Square; Ⓥ

With keen Buddhist leanings, this is one of Shanghai's superior spots for a vegetarian banquet. Realistic mock-meat is on the menu, so half the experience is experimenting. Gnaw on a deep-fried sparrow, chomp the charcoal grilled lamb with spice power or the spicy-yet-sweet sautéd shred meat with chilli sauce, and wonder why you ever bothered with real meat.

🍴 JEAN GEORGES 法国餐厅
Fusion   YYY

☎ 6321 7733; 4th fl, Three on the Bund, 3 E Zhongshan No 1 Rd; 中山东一路3号外滩3号4楼; ⏰ 11.30am-2.30pm & 6-11pm; Ⓜ E Nanjing Rd

Divine palate-pleasers (beef tenderloin in a miso-red-wine sauce, crab with mango and cumin crisps) are the order of the day at the Manhattan chef's sensuous Shanghai outpost. It's divided into casual and formal (set dinner only, Y538) dining rooms at night. Reserve.

🍴 M ON THE BUND
Continental   YYY

☎ 6350 9988; 7th fl, 20 Guangdong Rd; 广东路20号7楼; ⏰ 11.30am-2.30pm & 6-10.30pm; Ⓜ E Nanjing Rd

Alfresco dining is a popular option

The first to pitch up on the waterfront in the closing years of the last millennium, Michelle Garnaut's winning M on the Bund restaurant remains as crisp as its white linen. The food is Continental (crispy suckling pig, magret de canard), complemented by a gorgeous art-deco interior and 7th-floor terrace. Reserve.

SHANGHAI GRANDMOTHER 上海姥姥
Chinese   YY
☎ 6321 6613; 70 Fuzhou Rd; 福州路 70号; Ⓜ E Nanjing Rd
This packed home-style eatery is within easy striking distance of the Bund and perfect for a casual

lunch or dinner. You can't go wrong with the classics here: the fried tomato and egg, Grandmother's braised pork and three-cup chicken will ease you into Shanghai dining.

SOUTH MEMORY 望湘园
Hunanese   YY
☎ 6360 2797; 6th fl, Hongyi Plaza, 299 E Nanjing Rd; 南京东路299号宏伊国际广场6楼; Ⓜ E Nanjing Rd
The standout choice in the popular Hongyi Plaza, this Hunan restaurant features tantalising spicy hotpots (bamboo shoots and smoked pork, Y48), which are served in a miniwok without broth. Arrive early for a window seat.

BEST BUND NOODLES

Ajisen (味千拉面; Hongyi Plaza, 299 E Nanjing Rd; 南京东路299号 宏伊国际广场; M E Nanjing Rd) Wildly popular chilli-infused Japanese noodles; pay upfront.

Wuyue Renjia (吴越人家; basement, 479 E Nanjing Rd; 南京东路 479号; M E Nanjing Rd) Big bowls of Jiangsu *mian* (noodles) in a traditional setting.

🍴 TIANDI 天地一家
Chinese   YYY

☎ 6329 7333; 3rd fl, Bund 6, 6 E Zhong-shan No 1 Rd; 中山东一路6号3楼; ⏲ 11.30am-2.30pm & 6-11pm; M E Nanjing Rd

Sultry jazz standards set the tone at this new Bund 6 restaurant, which boasts an enticing, if un-likely, Beijing–Cantonese culinary pairing. Duck breast with mango and sweet-and-sour prawns are among the highlights. Reserve a table.

🍴 YANG'S FRY DUMPLINGS
小杨生煎馆 *Dumplings*   Y

101 Huanghe Rd; 黄河路101号; M People's Square

Order at the left counter then join the queue to pick up your order of scalding hot sesame-seed-and-scallion-coated dumplings.

🍴 YUNNAN ROAD FOOD STREET
云南南路美食街 *Diverse*   Y

South Yunnan Rd; 云南南路; M People's Square

This is just the spot for an authen-tic meal after museum-hopping at People's Square. Look out for Shaanxi dumplings at No 15, Uighur kebabs next door and five-fragrance dim sum at No 28. It's slated to expand into a night market in 2010.

🍸 DRINK

🍸 BAR ROUGE *Bar*

☎ 6339 1199; 7th fl, Bund 18, 18 E Zhongshan No 1 Rd; 外滩18号7楼; ⏲ 6pm-2am Sun-Thu, 6pm-4.30am Fri & Sat; M E Nanjing Rd

Bathed in ruby-red and blue light and subdued by chill-out music and dazzling Pudong terrace views, high-profile Bar Rouge aims its seductive formula and superb cocktails at the moneyed crowd and 20-something fashionistas.

🍸 BARBAROSSA 芭芭露莎会
所餐厅 *Bar*

☎ 6318 0220; People's Park, 231 W Nan-jing Rd; 南京西路231号, 人民公园 内; ⏲ 11am-2am; M People's Square

The implausible Moroccan vibe of this secluded bar eagerly taps into Shanghai's eclectic desires. Its inviting ground-floor dining area gives way to an oasis of scattered cushions, hookah pipes and a terrace bar upstairs, and the music is set to chill. Target happy hour (5pm to 8pm) to elude staggering prices.

☏ BUND 12 CAFÉ 外滩12号咖啡厅 *Cafe*

☎ 6329 5896; Room 226, 2nd fl, 12 E Zhongshan No 1 Rd; 中山东一路12号2楼226室; ⏱ 8am-7pm; Ⓜ E Nanjing Rd
With a lovely terrace and an inimitable location within the HSBC Building (p42), this charming cafe is a soothingly civilised coffee

spot when the Bund munchies and caffeine withdrawal need sating.

☏ CAPTAIN'S BAR 船长青年酒吧 *Bar*

☎ 6323 7869; 6th fl, 37 Fuzhou Rd; 福州路37号6楼; ⏱ 11am-2am; Ⓜ E Nanjing Rd
There's the odd drunken sailor, and the crummy lift needs updating here at the Captain's Bar. But it is a fine Bund-side terrace-equipped bar for phosphorescent Pudong views – as long as rubbing shoulders with the preening

Cocktails at Bar Rouge

glitterati and the desperate-to-impress isn't a must.

Y GLAMOUR BAR 魅力酒吧 *Bar*
☎ 6329 3751; 6th fl, 20 Guangdong Rd; 广东路20号6楼; ⏰ 5pm-2am Sun-Thu, 5pm-late Fri & Sat; M E Nanjing Rd
Comfortably gorgeous, Michelle Garnaut's bar moved down a floor from her restaurant above, and up the wish list of Shanghai socialites. A steady flow of elegant people enjoy tantalising martinis at the window seats midweek, avoiding the weekend crush. It also hosts film screenings, the annual literary festival, chamber music perform-ances and China-related book launches.

Y NEW HEIGHTS 新视角 *Bar, Restaurant*
☎ 6321 0909; 7th fl, Three on the Bund, 3 E Zhongshan No 1 Rd; 中山东一路3号外滩3号7楼; ⏰ 11am-1.30am; M E Nanjing Rd
The most amenable of the big Bund bars, this splendid ter-race has the choicest angle on Pudong's hypnotising neon performance.

★ PLAY

CABARET *Jazz*
Bund 6, 6 E Zhongshan No 1 Rd; 中山东一路6号; ⏰ 9pm-late; M E Nanjing Rd
The velvet curtains and pillow-laden couches are good for an atmospheric nightcap, but the live jazz is hit or miss.

M1NT *Club*
☎ 6391 2811; 24th fl, 318 Fuzhou Rd; 福州路318号24楼; ⏰ lounge 11.30am-late daily, club 10pm-late Fri & Sat; M E Nanjing Rd
Exclusive penthouse-style club with knockout views, snazzy food and not a lot of dance space. Dress to impress or you'll get thrown into the shark tank.

SHANGHAI CONCERT HALL 上海音乐厅 *Classical Music*
☎ 6386 2836; 523 E Yan'an Rd; 延安东路523号; M People's Square
Equipped with fine acoustics, this 75-year-old building is the venue for regular concerts by local and international orchestras and soloists.

SHANGHAI GRAND THEATRE 上海大剧院 *Classical Music*
☎ 6386 8686; 300 Renmin Ave; 人民大道300号; M People's Square
Shanghai's state-of-the-art concert venue hosts everything from Broadway musicals to symphonies, ballets, operas and perform-ances by internationally acclaimed classical soloists. There are also traditional Chinese music perform-ances here. You can pick up a show schedule at the ticket office.

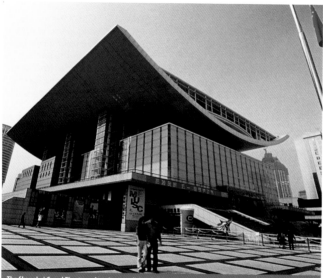

The Shanghai Grand Theatre: a hat tip to traditional Chinese architecture

⭐ YIFU THEATRE 逸夫舞台
Chinese Opera

☎ 6322 5294; www.tianchan.com; 701 Fuzhou Rd; 福州路701号; Ⓜ People's Square

Just east of People's Square, this theatre stands out with its huge opera mask above the entrance. On the program is Beijing opera, Kunqu and Yueju opera, with a Beijing opera highlights show performed several times a week at 1.30pm and 7.15pm. Tickets range from Y30 to Y380.

WALKING TOUR
THE BUND

This comprehensive walk can be done either by day or night. During the evening the buildings are closed but the views to Pudong are fantastic.

North of Suzhou Creek rises the brick pile of **Broadway Mansions (1)**, built in 1934 as an exclusive apartment block. Just across Huangpu Rd from the **Russian consulate (2)** is the distinguished **Astor House Hotel (3)**. Opened in 1846, this was

distance 1.3km **duration** 1½ hours
▶ **start** Broadway Mansions ● **end**
Meteorological Signal Tower

Shanghai's first hotel. Head south
over Waibaidu Bridge (formerly
Garden Bridge), which dates from
1907 and was actually removed
in 2008 for a year-long renovation
project. Walk down the west side
of the steel bridge and examine
the **political slogan (4)** from the Cultural Revolution era (1966–76).

Pass Huangpu Park (p42), stop-
ping in to look at the old photos

in the **Bund History Museum (5**; p42).
On the other side of the road is
the former headquarters of early
opium traders **Jardine Matheson (6)**
at No 27. The imposing **Bank of
China Building (7**; p39), at No 23, was
built in 1937 and was originally
designed to surpass the adjacent
Peace Hotel in height. But the
Bund's landmark remains Victor
Sassoon's **Peace Hotel (8**; p42), once
the most luxurious hotel in Asia.

Originally the Chartered Bank
of Australia, India and China,
Bund 18 (9) is a recent high-profile
conversion. Seventh-floor Bar
Rouge (p48) is only open in the
evening, but has excellent views
of Pudong and the straining Atlas
figures holding up the roof of
the adjacent former home of the
North China Daily News (10; No 17),
once the main English-language
newspaper in China.

Three buildings down, at No 13,
the **Customs House (11**; p39) was built
in 1925. Capping the building was
the largest clock face in Asia and
the 'Big Ching', a bell modelled
on London's Big Ben. Next door,
the **Hongkong & Shanghai Banking
Corporation (HSBC) Building (12**; p42)
was constructed in 1923, when
it was the second-largest bank in
the world.

Passing the luxury retail and
restaurant developments at Nos 9,
6, 5 and 3 brings you to the city's

most famous bastion of British snobbery, the former **Shanghai Club** (**13**; No 2). Its most famous accoutrement was its bar – at 33m, it was thought at one time to be the longest in the world.

Past the McBain Building at No 1 is the Meteorological Signal Tower, originally built in 1908 opposite the French consulate and now housing the modest **Bund Museum** (**14**; p39).

>OLD TOWN

Many Chinese cities have their old towns, where the original settlement began. Shanghai's Old Town, known to locals as Nan Shi (Southern City), is an intriguing area of old-fashioned textures, tatty charm and musty temples, and is a favourite stop for visitors. The circular layout still reflects the footprint of the former city walls, flung up in the 16th century to defend against marauding Japanese pirates. Today, sitting as it does on a piece of coveted real estate, and with many inhabitants considering the buildings old and rundown, it is not surprising that much of the area has been bulldozed to provide room for developers to build upwards. But for glimpses of old Shanghai, the remaining Old Town backstreets with their crowded lanes, dark alleyways and hanging laundry are the places to explore. The most interesting areas to wander are off the beaten track – try the alleys east of the Yuyuan Gardens (Anren St, 安仁街; Wutong Rd, 梧桐路; Danfeng Rd, 丹凤路) or north of the Confucius Temple.

OLD TOWN

◎ SEE
Chenxiangge Nunnery ..1 C2
Confucius Temple 2 B4
Dajing Pavilion 3 A2
Temple of the Town
    God 4 C2
Yuyuan Gardens 5 C2

🏠 SHOP
Dongtai Road
    Antique Market 6 A3

Fuyou Antique Market ..7 C2
Old Street 8 C2
Shiliupu Fabric Market ..9 D2
Yuyuan Bazaar 10 C2

🍴 EAT
Dragon Gate Mall 11 C2
Nanxiang Steamed Bun
    Restaurant 12 C2
Songyuelou 13 C2

▼ DRINK
Fat Olive 14 A3
Old Shanghai
    Teahouse 15 C2

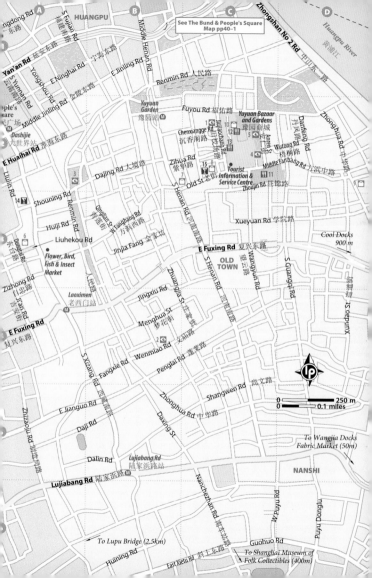

S Fujian Rd 福建南路

S Yunnan Rd 云南南路

Yongshou Rd 永寿路

Yan'an Rd 延安东路

S Yunnan Rd

Middle Jinling Rd 金陵中路

People's Square
人民广场

Dashijie
大世界

E Huaihai Rd 淮海东路

Liujin Rd 柳津路

Shouning Rd 寿宁路

Renmin Rd 人民路

Huiji Rd 会稽路

Liuhekou Rd

Zizhong Rd 自忠路

Jinan Rd 济南路

E Fuxing Rd 复兴东路

E Ninghai Rd 宁海东路

E Jinling Rd 金陵东路

Renmin Rd 人民路

Yuyuan
Garden
豫园游

Fuyou Rd 福佑路

Chenxiangge Rd
沉香阁路

Zihua Rd 紫华路

Dajing Rd 大境路

Qinglian Rd 青莲街

W Fangbang Rd 方浜西路

Jinjia Fang 金家坊

J.nxiu Rd
Jingxiu Rd

Renmin Rd 人民路

S Henan Rd 河南南路

Old St 老街

Zhuangjia St 庄家街

Menghua St
梦花街

Wenmiao Rd 文庙路

Fangxie Rd

Penglai Rd 蓬莱路

S Xizang Rd 西藏南路

E Jianguo Rd 建国东路

Daji Rd 大吉路

Zhonghua Rd 中华路

Daxing St 大兴街

Dalin Rd 大林路

Lujiabang Rd
陆家浜路站

Zhizaoju Rd 制造局路

Lujiabang Rd 陆家浜路

Nanchezhan Rd 南车站路

Huining Rd 会宁路

East Xietu Rd 斜土东路

S Xizang Rd

Yuyuan Bazaar
and Gardens
豫园商城

Anren St 安仁街

Jiujiaochang Rd 旧校场路

Zhonghua Rd 中华路

Danfeng Rd 丹凤路

Wutong Rd 梧桐路

Middle Fanbang Rd 方浜中路

Zhoujin Rd 芳馆路

Xueyuan Rd 学院路

Wangyun Rd 望云路

S Guangqi Rd 光启南路

S Xundao St

Shangwen Rd 尚文路

Tourist
Information &
Service Centre

OLD
TOWN

E Fuxing Rd 复兴东路

Flower, Bird,
Fish & Insect
Market

Laoximen
老西门站

E Fuxing Rd
复兴东路

Zhongshan No 2 Rd 中山东二路

Huangpu River

Huangpu Rd 黄浦江

Zhonghua Rd 中华路

NANSHI

W Puyu Rd

Wai Dongtai Rd

Guohuo Rd

Cool Docks
900 m

To Wangjia Docks
Fabric Market (50m)

To Lupu Bridge (2.5km)

To Shanghai Museum of
Folk Collectibles (400m)

0   250 m
0   0.1 miles

SEE

CHENXIANGGE NUNNERY 沉香阁

29 Chenxiangge Rd; 沉香阁路**29**号**; admission Y5;** 7am-4pm; M **Yuyuan Garden**
Seek out the tidy floral courtyard at the rear of this delightful retreat of muttered prayers and brown-clothed Buddhist nuns to climb the **Guanyin Tower** (观音楼; admission Y2; 7am-3pm), housing a compassionate effigy of Guanyin, carved from *chenxiang* wood and seated in *lalitasana* posture.

CONFUCIUS TEMPLE 文庙

215 Wenmiao Rd; 文庙路**215**号**; admission Y10;** 9am-5pm; M **Laoximen**
This well-tended shrine to Kongfuzi (Confucius) is pleasantly cultivated with hectacres of pines, magnolias and birdsong. The temple is typically Confucian (introspective, retiring, quiet), but a busy second-hand book market of (largely Chinese-language) books gets going every Sunday morning.

DAJING PAVILION 大境阁

Dajing Rd; 大境路**; admission Y5;** 9am-4pm; M **Dashijie**
Dating from 1815, this pavilion is attached to the sole preserved (and restored) section of the Old Town wall, which was toppled in 1912. On the ground floor is a Chinese-language exhibition of the Old Town and you can climb the battlements.

TEMPLE OF THE TOWN GOD 城隍庙

Middle Fangbang Rd; 方浜中路**; admission Y10;** 8.30am-4.30pm; M **Yuyuan Garden**
Chinese towns traditionally had a community of Taoist gods (often presided over by a main town god), who kept the populace from

---

SIGHTS JUST OUT OF OLD TOWN

Lupu Bridge (卢浦大桥; 905 Luban Rd; 鲁班路905号; admission Y68; M Luban Rd, then 17) For aerial views of the World Expo grounds and the city sprawl, climb up to a viewing platform at the apex of this suspension bridge. The entrance is located at the end of Luban Rd (under the bridge).
Shanghai Museum of Folk Collectibles (上海民间收藏品陈列馆; ☎ 6313 5582; 1551 S Zhongshan Rd; 中山南路1551号; admission Y4; 9am-4pm; M S Xi-zang Rd) Located at the northern edge of the World Expo site and housed in the magnificent Sanshan Guildhall (1909), this fascinating museum allows an exploration of Shanghai via the medium of collectibles, from cigarette lighters to ceramics and cruelly exquisite--looking miniature shoes for bound feet. A brand new wing was set to open in 2010.

Tao Wansheng
Tao, now 60, has worked as a traditional woodcarver since age 14, often undertaking temple restorations. He grew up in Pudong's farmland.

How much do you earn per month? Just enough to get by. But let me tell you, as I get older, money is not that important. The most important thing for me now is to cultivate myself through Buddhism and Taoism. **Do you think other Shanghainese are religious?** Yes. Most Shanghainese believe in Taoism and Buddhism. But really, Buddhism is too complicated for anyone to truly understand. **What do you consider to be a distinguishing feature of Shanghai?** It has always been a place where Chinese culture and Western culture have come together. The artwork here also used to be incredible – more impressive than in Beijing. But it was mostly destroyed in the Cultural Revolution.

NEIGHBOURHOODS

OLD TOWN

harm. This temple originally dated to the early 15th century before being badly damaged during the Cultural Revolution. Seek out the multifaith hall dedicated to three female deities, Guanyin (Buddhist), and Tianhou and Yanmu Niang niang (both Taoist).

ⓒ YUYUAN GARDENS 豫园
Yuyuan Bazaar; admission Y30;
⏰ **8.30am-5.30pm (last entry 5pm);**
Ⓜ **Yuyuan Garden**
Founded between 1559 and 1577 by the Pan family, these classical Chinese gardens (see also p22) were ransacked during both the Opium War and the Taiping Rebellion. This is a fine example of Ming dynasty garden design and highlights include the Three Ears of Corn Hall, the Exquisite Jade Rock, the Hall or Heralding Spring, and the gilded woodwork of the Ancient Stage.

🛍 SHOP
⌂ COOL DOCKS 时尚老码头
Fashion
479 S Zhongshan Rd; 中山南路479号;
Ⓜ **Xiaonanmen**
A recent development project often billed as Xintiandi 2, the Cool Docks, east of the Old Town, consist of several *shikumen* (stone-gate houses) surrounded by red-brick warehouses near the waterfront. Most of the shops and restaurants

had still failed to take off as 'in' destinations as we went to press.

⌂ DONGTAI ROAD ANTIQUE MARKET 东台路古玩市场
Antiques
☎ **5582 5254; Dongtai Rd;** 东台路;
⏰ **9am-6pm;** Ⓜ **Laoximen**
Picking up a genuine antique here is the proverbial needle in a haystack but there's a tremendous variety among the mass-produced Mao memorabilia and other predictable clutter on Dongtai Rd and Liuhekou Rd; haggle hard.

⌂ FUYOU ANTIQUE MARKET 福佑工艺品市场 *Antiques*
459 Middle Fangbang Rd; 方浜中路
459号; Ⓜ **Yuyuan Garden**
There's a permanent antique market here on the 1st and 2nd floors, but the place really gets humming for the 'ghost market' on Sunday at dawn, when sellers from the countryside fill up all four floors and then some.

⌂ OLD STREET 老街 *Souvenirs*
Middle Fangbang Rd; 方浜中路;
Ⓜ **Yuyuan Garden**
The morass of Mao-era keepsakes brings no surprises, but the ye olde China streetscape of Old Street is entertaining. Vendors are tamer than at Yuyuan Bazaar, and there's a glut of souvenirs: shadow puppets, calendar posters, Yixing

teapots, Tibetan jewellery, calligraphy scrolls and kites.

🏠 SHILIUPU FABRIC MARKET
十六铺面料城 *Fabric, Fashion*

☎ 6330 1043; 2 Zhonghua Rd; 中华路2号; 🕑 8.30am-6.30pm; Ⓜ Xiaonanmen

Browse for cheap silks (Y200 per metre or less), cashmere, wool, linen and cotton, but watch you don't wind up with a synthetic. Tailored clothing is a steal if you've a cashmere coat, silk shirt or traditional Chinese jacket on your shopping list – count on one to three days' turnaround.

🏠 WANGJIA DOCKS FABRIC MARKET 王家码头丝绸面料市场 *Fabric*

191 Nancang St; 南仓街191号; 🕑 8.30am-6pm

Those in the market for a luxurious silk quilt (comforter; 蚕丝被) should make the trek south to this fascinating neighbourhood, awash in tailors and fabric dealers. Quilts are sold by weight and size – figure on about Y650 for a queen-sized quilt weighing 2kg.

🏠 YUYUAN BAZAAR 豫园商城
Souvenirs

Fuyou Rd; Ⓜ Yuyuan Garden

You never get inured to the shrieks of 'hello, hello, yes, watch, bags' and 'make it cheaper for you', but shopping here is entertaining. Join the crowds surrounding the *layangpian* (拉洋片) performer, don't forget to snack, and pay your respects at the Temple of the Town God.

🍴 EAT

🍴 DRAGON GATE MALL
豫龙坊 *Food Court*   Y–YYY

Middle Fangbang Rd; 方浜中路; 🕑 9am-11pm; Ⓜ Yuyuan Garden

True, eating in a mall isn't *quite* the same as wandering amid the

---

SAFETY

Shanghai is a very safe city, but observing some simple rules can save heartache:

> Make sure you keep your money in inside pockets. Markets such as Qipu Rd (p107) are often crawling with thieves, some of whom surround you pretending they are there to sell you something.
> Keep a close eye on your Y100 notes. They can be cannily swapped for a fake and then handed back to you as 'unacceptable'.
> When boarding the metro, don't force yourself on after the alarm has sounded. A man was killed in 2007 when the outer security doors closed before the carriage doors, trapping him.

chaos of the Yuyuan Bazaar, but if you've had enough of the push and pull of the crowds, the selection of restaurants here is a lifesaver. The enormous dragon-arch fountain marks the entrance.

🍴 NANXIANG STEAMED BUN RESTAURANT 南翔馒头店
Dumplings   *YY*

85 Old Yuyuan Rd, Yuyuan Bazaar; 豫园商城豫园老路85号; ⏰ **10am-9pm;** Ⓜ **Yuyuan Garden**

Shanghai's most celebrated pork and crabmeat *xiaolongbao* (steamed dumplings) eatery is alas hugely popular – the takeaway queue emerging from the door

Nanxiang Steamed Bun Restaurant

says it all. Minimum Y60 per person eat-in charge.

🍴 SONGYUELOU 松月楼
Chinese   *Y*

99 Jiujiaochang Rd; 旧校场路99号; ⏰ **7am-7.30pm;** Ⓜ **Yuyuan Garden;** Ⓥ

Shanghai's oldest vegie restaurant (dating back to 1910), this place offers a far more authentic dining experience than most of the tourist-saturated restaurants in the area. English menus upstairs.

🍸 DRINK

🍸 FAT OLIVE *Bar*
☎ **6334 3288; 6th fl, 228 S Xizang Rd;** 西藏南路228号6楼; ⏰ **11am-1am;** Ⓜ **Dashijie;** 📶

The brainchild of chef David Laris, the Fat Olive serves Greek-style mezze accompanied by a good selection of New World wines. It's nestled among office towers with a cosy outdoor deck overlooking the Old Town. Enter through the Fraser Residence on Shouning Rd.

🍸 OLD SHANGHAI TEAHOUSE 老上海茶馆 *Teahouse*
☎ **5382 1202; 385 Middle Fangbang Rd;** 方浜中路385号; ⏰ **9am-9pm;** Ⓜ **Yuyuan Garden**

Dropping in on this upstairs teahouse is much like barging into

2010 WORLD EXPO

In terms of economic and social impact, the World Expo (世博会) is the third-largest event on the planet after the Olympic Games and the FIFA World Cup. The Shanghai government directed a staggering US$4.2 billion towards hosting the Expo, which is expected to attract 70 million visitors, making it the largest in the event's almost 160-year-old history. While the central theme of sustainable urban development is certainly an apt one for China, the Expo's most immediate effects are at the infrastructure level. Subway line extensions, new river ferry services, a new river tunnel, and a complete makeover of Shanghai's world-famous esplanade, the Bund, will all be lasting legacies – as well as the controversial relocation of an estimated 18,000 families. Most of the participating countries' pavilions are designed to be temporary and will be dismantled by May 2011 at the latest, but five eye-catching permanent structures will remain: the China Pavilion, the Expo Boulevard, the Themes Pavilion, the World Expo Centre and the Expo Performance Centre. It is assumed that they will continue to host events after the Expo has finished.

> **When** 1 May to 31 October 2010.
> **Where** The World Expo site straddles the Huangpu River between Nanpu Bridge and Lupu Bridge in the south of town. Most of the site will be in Pudong district, and will be linked to the rest of the city by new ferry services and subway lines 7, 8 and 13.
> **How much** Tickets cost Y160 for one day, except on peak days when they cost Y200.
> **Stuff to do** Most participating countries will have specially made pavilions showcasing their cultural, economic and technological strengths. As well as being able to judge which looks the coolest, visitors can also peruse interactive exhibitions and watch performances. More than 100 different shows per day are planned.
> **Further information** Call the hot line (☎ 962 010 or visit the website (http://en.expo2010.cn)

someone's attic, where ancient gramophones, records, typewriters and other period clutter shares space with the aroma of Chinese tea. Refillable cups of various Chinese teas from Y35.

>FRENCH CONCESSION EAST

For full immersion in Shanghai's most chic and fashionable charms, there's little need to stray from the French Concession. Once home to the lion's share of Shanghai's adventurers, radicals, gangsters, writers, prostitutes and pimps, Shanghai's very reputation as the 'Paris of the East' evolved from the French Concession's tree-lined streets and European villas. Today, the neighbourhood has retained its chic charms while eradicating its more dissolute tendencies. After ticking the Bund and People's Square boxes, your Shanghai needs – shopping, dining, drinking and sleeping – can all be met here. The French Concession East – the eastern half of this European-style neighbourhood also known as Frenchtown – is closest to the heart of Shanghai. Off the main haul of Huaihai Rd, the shady, low-rise streets exude an unrushed personality deeply at odds with the unrelenting sky-rise nature of Pudong or the uniform sprawl of the suburbs.

FRENCH CONCESSION EAST

SEE
Art Labor 1 C4
Cathay Theatre 2 C2
Fuxing Park 3 E2
Jinjiang Hotel 4 C2
Moller House 5 B1
ShanghART 6 D2
Shikumen Open House
  Museum 7 F2
Site of the 1st National
  Congress of the CCP ...8 F2
St Nicholas Church 9 D3
Sun Yatsen's Former
  Residence 10 E3
Taikang Road Art
  Centre & Tianzifang ..11 E5
Xintiandi 12 F2

SHOP
100 Change & Insect ...13 B2
Cybermart 14 G1

Heping Finery 15 C3
Huifeng Tea Shop 16 C3
Insh 17 E5
Junmeizu 18 B2
Shanghai Tang 19 C2
Shirt Flag 20 C3
Springhead 21 E5
Taikang Rd Art Centre.. (see 11)
The Thing 22 B2
Xintiandi ....(see 12)

EAT
Crystal Jade 23 F2
Di Shui Dong 24 C2
Din Tai Fung ....(see 23)
Dongbei Ren 25 B1
Kommune 26 E5
Southern Barbarian 27 C1
T8 ....28 F2
Uighur Restaurant......(see 25)
Vegetarian Lifestyle 29 G1
Ye Shanghai 30 F2

DRINK
Citizen Café 31 C1
Dr Bar ....(see 30)
TMSK ....(see 28)

PLAY
Babyface 32 G1
Melting Pot 33 E5
Partyworld 34 E2
Shanghai Conservatory
  of Music 35 B3

Please see over for map

👁 SEE

👁 FUXING PARK 复兴公园
admission free; 🕐 **5am-6pm;** Ⓜ Ⓢ **Shanxi Rd or Xintiandi**
Laid out by the French in 1909, this lovely, leafy park is a European antidote to Shanghai's brood of synthetic parks. There's always much to see, whether it be slow-motion taichi types or chess players hunched over their boards in the shade of towering *wutong* trees.

👁 SHANGHART 香格纳画廊
☎ **3395 0808; www.shanghart.com; 796 Middle Huaihai Rd;** 淮海中路796号; **admission free;** 🕐 **10am-7pm;** Ⓜ Ⓢ **Shanxi Rd**
The 1920s twin villas and garden (formerly the residence of a Shanghai middleman or *comprador*) houses a gorgeous new branch of Shanghai's most established contemporary art gallery.

👁 SHIKUMEN OPEN HOUSE MUSEUM 石库门屋里厢
☎ **3307 0337; Xintiandi North Block, No 25, Lane 181 Taicang Rd;** 太仓路181弄25号楼新天地北里; **admission Y20;** 🕐 **10.30am-10.30pm Sun-Thu, 11am-11pm Fri & Sat;** Ⓜ Ⓢ **Huangpi Rd or Xintiandi**
An invitingly arranged and restored two-storey *shikumen* (stone-gate house) within Xintiandi (p66), decorated with period furniture and infused with the

Shikumen Open House Museum

charms of yesteryear Shanghai. Peek into the minute, wedge-shaped *tingzijian* room on the landing, which used to be rented out to cash-strapped writers and other penurious tenants.

👁 SITE OF THE 1ST NATIONAL CONGRESS OF THE CCP 中共一大会址纪念馆
☎ **5383 2171; Xintiandi North Block, 76 Xingye Rd;** 兴业路76号; **admission free;** 🕐 **9am-5pm (last entry 4pm);** Ⓜ Ⓢ **Huangpi Rd or Xintiandi**
The communist narcissism and back-slapping might be irritating to some people, but this lovely *shikumen* house is immortalised as one of China's

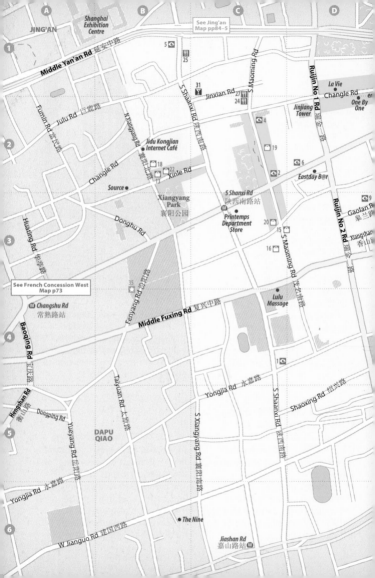

JING'AN

Shanghai Exhibition Centre

See Jing'an
Map pp84–5

Middle Yan'an Rd 延安中路

Fumin Rd 富民路

Julu Rd 巨鹿路

N Xiangyang Rd 襄阳北路

S Shaanxi Rd 陕西南路

Jinxian Rd

Maoming Rd

Ruijin No 1 Rd 瑞金一路

La Vie

Changle Rd

One By One

Changle Rd

Jidu Kongjian
Internet Café

Jinjiang
Tower

Xinle Rd

Source

Eastday B@r

Huating Rd 华亭路

Xiangyang
Park 襄阳公园

Donghu Rd

S Shanxi Rd
陕西南路站

Ruijin No 2 Rd 瑞金二路

Gaolan Rd
皋兰路

Xiangshan R
香山路

Printemps
Department
Store

S Maoming Rd 茂名南路

See French Concession West
Map p73

Fenyang Rd 汾阳路

Middle Fuxing Rd 复兴中路

M Changshu Rd
常熟路站

Lulu
Massage

Baoging Rd 宝庆路

Hengshan Rd 衡山路

Dongping Rd

Yueyang Rd 岳阳路

Taiyuan Rd 太原路

DAPU
QIAO

Yongjia Rd 永嘉路

S Xiangyang Rd 襄阳南路

S Shaanxi Rd 陕西南路

Shaoxing Rd 绍兴路

Yongjia Rd 永嘉路

W Jianguo Rd 建国西路

The Nine

Jiashan Rd
嘉山路站 **M**

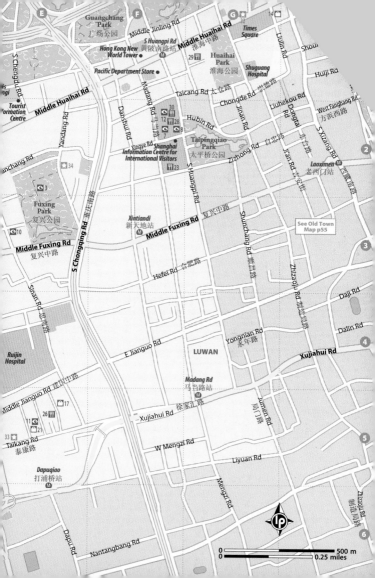

al shrines, where
..... Communist Party
(CCP) was founded on 23 July
1921, with a youthful Mao Zedong
in attendance.

🄲 ST NICHOLAS CHURCH 圣尼
古拉斯教堂

**16 Gaolan Rd; 皋兰路16号; M S
Huangpi Rd**

This now-derelict Russian Ortho-
dox church was built to service
the huge influx of Russians who
arrived in Shanghai in the 1930s.
It was spared destruction during
the Cultural Revolution by a
portrait of Mao Zedong, hung
strategically from its dome. It was
not open to the public at press
time.

🄲 SUN YATSEN'S FORMER
RESIDENCE 孙中山故居

**☎ 6437 2954; 7 Xiangshan Rd; 香山路
7号; admission Y20; 🕙 9am-4pm; M S
Shanxi Rd or Xintiandi**

Sun Yatsen (1866–1925), the father
of modern China, dwelled in this
two-storey house on Rue Molière
from 1918 to 1924. It's a simple
and retiring slice of Sun Yatsen
nostalgia and memorabilia.

🄲 TAIKANG ROAD ART
CENTRE & TIANZIFANG 太康路
艺术中心、田子坊

**210 Taikang Rd; 太康路210弄;
M Dapuqiao**

FRENCH CONCESSION ART GALLERIES

A handful of contemporary art galleries
have set up in intimate French Concession spaces. In addition to ShanghART
(p63), hunt down the following two.
Art Labor (☎ 6431 7782; www.art
laborgallery.com; 10-36 Yongjia Rd; 永
嘉路36-10号; 🕙 11am-7pm Tue-
Sat, noon-6pm Sun; M S Shanxi Rd)
James Cohan (Map p73, D5; ☎ 5466
0825; www.jamescohan.com; Bldg 1,
Lane 170, Yueyang Rd; 岳阳路170弄
1号楼; 🕙 10am-6pm Tue-Sat, noon-
6pm Sun; M Hengshan Rd)

A hub of design studios, wi-fi cafes
and cool boutiques, this charming
alleyway complex (see also p18) is
the perfect antidote to Shanghai's
oversized malls. Families still reside
in neighbouring buildings and a
community mood survives.

🄲 XINTIANDI 新天地

**cnr Taicang & Madang Rds; 太仓路
与马当路路口; M S Huangpi Rd or
Xintiandi**

A Shanghai icon, Xintiandi is the
French Concession's thriving
shikumen rebuild (see also p19),
where trendy dining, drinking,
retail and sightseeing converge.

🛍 SHOP

In addition to the shops listed on
the following pages, there are

great boutique streets in this area. See p126 for more information.

🔲 100 CHANGE & INSECT 百变虫鞋专卖店 *Shoes*

☎ 5404 0767; 76 Xinle Rd; 新乐路76号; ⏱ 10.30am-10pm; Ⓜ S Shanxi Rd

Strange name, funky footwear – for those who want their heels to be seen in the dark.

🔲 CYBERMART 赛博数码广场 *Electronics*

1 Middle Huaihai Rd; 淮海中路1号; ⏱ 10am-8pm; Ⓜ Dashijie

The most central and reliable location for all sorts of gadgetry, including memory sticks, mp3 players, laptops and digital cameras. Bargain, but don't expect enormous discounts.

🔲 HEPING FINERY 和平旗袍专卖店 *Fashion*

☎ 6473 9043; 161 S Maoming Rd; 茂名南路161号; ⏱ 9.30am-9.30pm; Ⓜ S Shanxi Rd

South Maoming Rd and Changle Rd are thick with small tailors where you can get sleeved in a *qipao* (cheongsam); this shop offers good value. Tailor-made *qipao* start at Y880, taking three days to make.

🔲 HUIFENG TEA SHOP 汇丰茶庄 *Tea*

☎ 6472 7196; 124 S Maoming Rd; 茂名南路124号; ⏱ 9am-9.30pm; Ⓜ S Shanxi Rd

A friendly, reliable tea shop, which has good-quality clay teapots, cups and a great range of Chinese tea. Sample varieties and make your choice, or try 50g of Iron Guanyin (铁观音) for Y20.

🔲 INSH 玩场 *Fashion*

☎ 6466 5249; Taikang Road Art Centre, No 11a, Lane 210; 泰康路210弄11a号; ⏱ 10.30am-9pm; Ⓜ Dapuqiao

Contemporary fashion (hats, T-shirts, jackets) with a bohemian twist, created by local designer Helen Lee.

🔲 SHANGHAI TANG 上海滩 *Fashion*

☎ 5466 3006; 59 S Maoming Rd; 茂名南路59号; ⏱ 10am-10pm; Ⓜ S Shanxi Rd

Shanghai Tang flies the flag for the Middle Kingdom in the world of high-end fashion. The designs are classic Chinese with a twist, incorporating fluorescent colours, traditional motifs and luxury fabrics.

🔲 SHIRT FLAG 衫旗帜 *Fashion*

☎ 5465 3011; 330 Nanchang Rd; 南昌路330号; ⏱ 10.30am-10pm; Ⓜ S Shanxi Rd

Fun, quality T-shirts, including its totemic angry panda series, which gives an ironic twist to Maoist propaganda. There are also branches in the Taikang Road Art Centre (p68) and M50 (p83).

🏠 **SPRINGHEAD** 根源
Handicrafts

☎ 6473 9837; Taikang Road Art Centre, No 17, Lane 274; 泰康路274弄17号田子坊; ◷ 9am-10pm; Ⓜ Dapuqiao

A handicrafts shop with an intriguing collection of folk-art prints as well as diaries, paper cuts and communist-era enamel mugs.

🏠 **TAIKANG ROAD ART CENTRE** 太康路艺术中心、田子坊
Fashion, Souvenirs

Taikang Rd; 太康路; Ⓜ Dapuqiao

The alleyways here are overflowing with unique boutiques, selling everything from yak-wool scarves to retro communist dinnerware. Stores to look out for include **Feel Shanghai** (Unit 110, No 3, Lane 210) for tailored Chinese clothing; **Esydragon** (No 20, Lane 210) for quirky souvenirs; **Chouchou Chic** (No 47, Lane 248) for children's clothing; and **Joma** (Unit 6, No 7, Lane 210) for Himalayan jewellery.

🏠 **XINTIANDI** 新天地 *Fashion, Souvenirs*

Cnr Taicang & Madang Rds; 太仓路与马当路路口; Ⓜ S Huangpi Rd or Xintiandi

The North Block is the best place to browse for local designer clothing. Look for embroidered accessories at **Annabel Lee** (Bldg 3), chic eco-friendly fabrics from **Shanghai Trio** (No 4, enter via Taicang Rd), iridescent glass creations at **Liuligongfang** (Bldg 11) and mod jewellery from **NoD** (Bldg 25).

🍴 EAT

🍴 **CRYSTAL JADE** 翡翠酒家
Dim Sum YY

☎ 6385 8752; Xintiandi South Block, 2nd fl, Bldg 6 (in the mall), Lane 123 Xingye Rd; 兴业路123弄新天地南里6号2楼; ◷ 11am-11pm; Ⓜ S Huangpi Rd or Xintiandi

What distinguishes Crystal Jade from other dim-sum restaurants

---

ART DECO SHANGHAI

If you're a lover of all things art deco, be sure to check out these beautiful examples of art-deco architecture (see also p15):

> The Metropole Hotel and Hamilton House (Map pp40–1, G3)
> The magnificent Park Hotel (Map pp40–1, C3), once the tallest building in Asia
> Nearby the Park Hotel stands the Grand Cinema (Map pp40–1, C3)
> The Cathay Theatre (Map pp64–5, C2) and Jinjiang Hotel (Map pp64–5, C2) in the French Concession
> The gigantesque abattoir 1933 (Map p105, D3)
> The Paramount Ballroom (p90).

is the dough: dumpling skins are perfectly tender, steamed buns come out light and airy, and the noodles are freshly made. Come for lunch; reservations are recommended.

DI SHUI DONG 滴水洞
Hunanese　　　　　　　　YY
☎ 6253 2689; 2nd fl, 56 S Maoming Rd; 茂名南路56号2楼; ◷ 10.30am-12.30am; M S Shanxi Rd
Named after a cave at Mao Zedong's birthplace, this Hunan eatery's low-key rustic charms are matched by a spicy menu. The claim to fame is the *ziran* (cumin) ribs, but don't miss out on winners such as spicy bean curd or 'Stewed Pork in Sauce of Chairman Mao's Style'.

DIN TAI FUNG 鼎泰丰
Dumplings　　　　　　　　YY
☎ 6385 8378; Xintiandi South Block, 2nd fl, Bldg 6 (in the mall), Lane 123 Xingye Rd; 兴业路123弄新天地南里6号楼2楼; ◷ 10am-midnight; M S Shanxi Rd or Xintiandi; V
If you love dumplings but aren't confident about eating street food, Din Tai Fung is your spot. Styles run from crinkled *shaomai* to Shanghai's steamed *xiaolong-bao* as well as wonton soup and vegetarian and other options. Reserve a table.

DONGBEI REN 东北人
Manchurian　　　　　　　　Y
☎ 5228 8288; 2nd fl, 1 S Shaanxi Rd; 陕西南路1号; ◷ 11am-2pm & 4.30-10pm; M S Shanxi Rd
It's lost a shot of vim, but this busy eatery still assures a fun night out. Hearty home cooking from northeast China (cumin lamb, stir-fried potato and eggplant, dumplings) and convivial waitresses in pigtails keep the crowds happy.

KOMMUNE 公社 *Cafe*　　YY
☎ 6466 2416; Taikang Road Art Centre, The Yard, No 7, Lane 210; 泰康路210弄7号田子坊; ◷ 8am-midnight; M Dapuqiao;
This popular Taikang Road Art Centre cafe offers a bank of internet terminals, big breakfasts and outside courtyard seating.

SOUTHERN BARBARIAN
南蛮子 *Yunnanese*　　　　YY
☎ 5157 5510; E7, 2nd fl, Life Art Gallery Space, 56 S Maoming Rd; 茂名南路56号生活艺术空间2楼E7; ◷ 11am-2.30pm & 5-10.30pm; M S Shanxi Rd
Fine, MSG-free Yunnan cuisine served in a laid-back (though somewhat noisy) atmosphere. Unusual dishes include the stewed beef and mint casserole, 'grandmother's mashed potatoes' and the addictive chicken wings. Booking a table is recommended.

🍴 **T8** *Fusion* YYY
☎ 6355 8999; Xintiandi North Block, Bldg 8, Lane 181; 太仓路181弄新天地北里8号楼; ⏰ 11.30am-2.30pm & 6.30-11.30pm; Ⓜ S Huangpi Rd or Xintiandi
The seductive grey-brick interior is the perfect setting for the delectable 'Mediterranean with Asian accents' menu (Sichuan high pie, tataki of sesame crusted tuna), taking diners and Shanghai celebs to new levels of irresistibility. Reservations are recommended.

🍴 **UIGHUR RESTAURANT** 维吾尔餐厅 *Uighur* Y
☎ 5228 8288; 1st fl, 1 S Shaanxi Rd; 陕西南路1号; Ⓜ S Shanxi Rd
Downstairs from Dongbei Ren, the Uighur does spicy lamb kebabs, nan bread and *polo* (rice pilaf) for a taste of Central Asia. There's also obligatory dancing to Radio Xinjiang's top 40, sung by the staff.

🍴 **VEGETARIAN LIFESTYLE** 枣子树 *Vegetarian, Chinese* YY
☎ 6384 8000; 77 Songshan Rd; 嵩山路77号; ⏰ 11am-9pm; Ⓜ S Huangpi Rd; Ⓥ
A branch of Shanghai's top vegie restaurant.

🍴 **YE SHANGHAI** 夜上海 *Shanghainese* YYY
☎ 6311 2323; Xintiandi North Block, 338 S Huangpi Rd; 黄陂南路338号新天地北里; ⏰ 11.30am-2.30pm & 6-10.30pm; Ⓜ S Shanxi Rd or Xintiandi

Ye offers sophisticated, unchallenging (ie few internal organs are on the menu) Shanghainese cuisine in classy 1930s-style surroundings. The drunken chicken and smoked fish are an excellent overture to mouthwatering main dishes, such as the crispy duck with pancakes. Reserve a table.

🍸 # DRINK

🍸 **CITIZEN CAFÉ** 天台餐厅 *Cafe*
☎ 6258 1620; 222 Jinxian Rd; 进贤路222号; ⏰ 11am-12.30am; Ⓜ S Shanxi Rd; 📶
Citizen's burgundy-and-cream colours, antique ceiling fans and well-worn parquet offer calming respite from the Shanghai crush. Recharge with a club sandwich or espresso or while away the evening over ginger cocktails.

🍸 **DR BAR** 木头咖啡吧 *Bar*
☎ 6311 0358; Xintiandi North Block, Bldg 15, Lane 181; 太仓路181弄新天地里15号楼; Ⓜ S Huangpi Rd or Xintiandi
The hipsters' hidden Xintiandi hangout, the excruciatingly neat DR Bar is all-black, pupil-dilating minimalist cool.

🍸 **TMSK** 透明思考 *Bar*
☎ 6326 2227; Xintiandi North Block, Bldg 11, Lane 181; 天仓路181弄新天地北里11号楼; ⏰ 11.30pm-1.30am; Ⓜ S Huangpi Rd or Xintiandi
A place to visit as much for the decor as for the drinks, TMSK is

designed to within an inch of its life; swirled iridescent glass sets the dazzling supercool ambiance. Check out the house band's unholy fusion of techno and traditional Chinese music (9pm-10pm Monday to Saturday).

⭐ PLAY

⭐ BABYFACE *Club*
☎ 6375 6667; Unit 101, Shanghai Sq, 138 Middle Huaihai Rd; 淮海中路138号101室; ⏰ 9pm-2am; Ⓜ S Huangpi Rd

Babyface may be a nationwide chain, but it's still one of the longest-running and least exclusive clubs in the city. The crowd is predominately local.

⭐ MELTING POT *Live Music*
☎ 6467 9900; 288 Taikang Rd; 泰康路288号; ⏰ 5.30pm-1am; Ⓜ Dapuqiao

The Melting Pot has an eclectic line-up of local musicians every night of the week, and the Taikang Rd locale means it's often hopping.

⭐ PARTYWORLD 钱柜 *Karaoke*
☎ 6374 1111; 109 Yandang Rd; 雁荡路109号, 复兴公园内; ⏰ 8am-2am; Ⓜ S Huangpi Rd

If you want to party it up in true Chinese style, then karaoke should top your list of night-time activities. This monster venue has plenty of English-language songs available.

LIVE MUSIC

Shanghai has a bad rep when it comes to live music, but the venues have improved dramatically in recent years. For home-grown rock, **Yuyintang** (育音堂; Map p73, A4; ☎ 5237 8662; www.yuyintang.org; 1731 W Yan'an Rd, 延安西路1731号; ⏰ 8pm-midnight Thu-Sun; Ⓜ W Yan'an Rd) and **Zhijiang Dream Factory** (芷江梦工场; Map pp84-5, D3; ☎ 5213 5086; New Factories, 4th fl, Bldg B, 28 Yuyao Rd; 余姚路28号同乐坊; ⏰ 8pm-1am; Ⓜ Changping Rd) are the best of the bunch. If traditional Chinese music is more your cup of *cha*, try **Bandu Cabin** (p90) or the **Oriental Art Center** (p97) on Saturdays. Jazz, a Shanghai standard in the 1930s, is on tap at the **Cotton Club** (p80) and **JZ Club** (p81), while dishy newcomers such as **Cabaret** (p50) occasionally throw a memorable party.

⭐ SHANGHAI CONSERVATORY OF MUSIC
上海音乐学院 *Classical Music*
☎ 6431 1792; 20 Fenyang Rd; 汾阳路20号; Ⓜ S Shanxi Rd

Enjoying a refurbishment at the time of writing, the conservatory stages student-performed classical and traditional Chinese music at 7.15pm every day. The **ticket office** (*shoupiaochu*; 售票处; ⏰ 9am-5pm) is in the southern part of campus.

>FRENCH CONCESSION WEST

Taking up from where the French Concession East left off, the French Concession West continues its picturesque meandering southwest to Jiaotong University and north to the busy sweep of West Nanjing Rd (p82). In between the two is an elegant treasure-trove of art-deco architecture, Concession-era villas, and all the charm of the French Concession's atmospheric back streets. As with the French Concession East, shopping, drinking and dining are a visitor's most natural inclinations here. The district is not strong on individual sights, but its sheer variety of shops, bars and restaurants – especially around Donghu Rd (off Middle Huaihai Rd) and Taojiang Rd (off Hengshan Rd) – coupled with its attractive Concession streetscapes and inviting tempo, make it one of the most stimulating parts of town.

FRENCH CONCESSION WEST

⊙ SEE
CY Tung Maritime
 Museum 1 A6
Propaganda Poster
 Art Centre 2 B3
Shanghai Museum of
 Arts & Crafts 3 D4
Song Qingling's Former
 Residence 4 B5

⌂ SHOP
Ba Yan Ka La 5 B5
Brocade Country 6 D2
Chinese Printed Blue
 Nankeen Exhibition
 Hall 7 D3
Madame Mao's Dowry ... 8 D3

Simply Life 9 D5
Skylight 10 C4
Spin 11 D2
Urban Tribe 12 C4

⑪ EAT
Azul/Viva/Vargas Grill .. 13 C4
Bai's Restaurant 14 C6
Baoluo Jiulou 15 D3
Ginger 16 B4
Haiku 17 D4
Jishi Jiulou 18 B5
Lost Heaven 19 B4
Noodle Bull 20 D3
Pinchuan 21 C4
Sichuan Citizen 22 D3

ⓨ DRINK
Abbey Road 23 D5
Boonna Café 24 D3
Boxing Cat Brewery 25 C4
Cotton's 26 C6
Little Face .... (see 22)
LOgO 27 A5
Velvet Lounge 28 C3
Zapata's 29 D5

★ PLAY
Cotton Club 30 C4
Dragon Club 31 D4
JZ Club 32 C4
Shanghai Fantasia 33 B3
Shelter 34 C4

SEE

CY TUNG MARITIME MUSEUM 董浩云航运博物馆

☎ 6293 3035; www.cytungmaritime
museum.com; Jiaotong University, 1954
Huashan Rd; 华山路1954号交通大
学内; admission free; ☽ 1.30-5.30pm
Tue-Sun; Ⓜ Jiaotong University

This small museum explores the
little-known world of Chinese
maritime history, with model
ships, maps of early trade routes
and exhibits on the legendary
Chinese Muslim seafarer Zheng He
and the maritime Silk Route.

PROPAGANDA POSTER ART CENTRE 宣传画黏画艺术中心

☎ 6211 1845; www.shanghaipropa
gandaart.com; Room B-OC, President
Mansion, 868 Huashan Rd; 华山路
868号; admission Y20; ☽ 10am-4.30pm;
Ⓜ Jiangsu Rd

With the Cultural Revolution still a
no-go zone for aspiring intellectu-
als and journalists, Shanghai distils
the cream of its Communist propaganda at this fascinating basement
museum and shop, where 3000
posters from Mao's heyday broad-
cast their unwavering message of
utopian bliss. Look out for the big

Mao and friends at the Propaganda Poster Art Centre

character posters *(dazibao)*, a rare and vanishing breed.

☉ SONG QINGLING'S FORMER RESIDENCE 宋庆龄故居

☎ 6474 7183; 1843 Middle Huaihai Rd; 淮海中路1843号; admission Y20; ☽ 9am-4.30pm; Ⓜ Jiatong University

Putting the dubious pebbledash exterior aside, this home to the wife of Sun Yatsen has historic charm. The English-style garden, with waxy-leaved *Magnolia grandiflora* and towering camphor trees, steals the show.

☉ SHANGHAI MUSEUM OF ARTS & CRAFTS 上海工艺美术博物馆

☎ 6437 2509; 79 Fenyang Rd; 汾阳路79号; admission Y8; ☽ 9am-4pm; Ⓜ Changshu Rd

Catch crafts emerging from the skilled fingers of on-site artisans, watch Chinese paper-cutting, embroidery and lacquer work and get your souvenir shopping sorted. The lovely building (built in 1905) and its gorgeous lawn are showpiece extras.

🛍 SHOP

🏛 BA YAN KA LA 巴颜喀拉
Body & Bath Products

☎ 6126 7600; Ferguson Lane Shopping Centre, Unit B1-b, 376 Wukang Rd; 武康路376号B1-b室; ☽ 10am-9pm; Ⓜ Shanghai Library

---

This well-conceived store offers a luxurious line of natural beauty products derived from Chinese herbal medicine. Goji berry (skin revitalisation), lotus seed (skin nourishment) and mulberry (detoxification) are the principal ingredients in the shampoos, bath salts, facial scrubs and scented candles.

🏛 BROCADE COUNTRY 锦绣纺
Handicrafts

☎ 6279 2677; 616 Julu Rd; 巨鹿路616号; ☽ 10.30am-7pm; Ⓜ Changshu Rd or Jing'an Temple

Peruse an exquisite collection of minority handicrafts from China's southwest, most of which are second-hand (ie not made for

Elfa Huang

A native Shanghainese, Elfa studied fashion design at university and opened a boutique on Changle Rd after graduating.

Do you think Shanghai is the most fashionable city in China? Of course! The young Shanghainese are more open to new ideas from other parts of the world. And women here can afford to care a lot about their appearance because we are more independent – we don't need to depend on men. **Who are your most common customers?** Young middle-class women – they often spend between Y700 and Y1000 (US$100 to US$146) at a time. But they're not necessarily from Shanghai; I'm seeing more and more customers from other provinces. **What do you do in your free time?** I go shopping! And sometimes I go dancing at Muse (p90). **If you could change one thing in Shanghai, what would it be?** Nothing! I'm quite satisfied with my life here.

the tourist trade) and personally selected by the owner Liu Xiaolan, a Guizhou native.

🏠 CHINESE PRINTED BLUE NANKEEN EXHIBITION HALL
中国蓝印花布馆 *Fabric*

☎ 5403 7947; No 24, Lane 637, Changle Rd; 长乐路637弄24号; ⏲ 9am-5pm; Ⓜ Changshu Rd

The spectacle here of bolts of indigo cloth drying in the summer sun is gorgeous. Surly staff aside, focus on the delightful blue-and-white cotton fabric, shoes, slippers, blouses, *qipao* (cheongsam) and small cloth bags. Follow the signs down the alley.

🏠 MADAME MAO'S DOWRY
毛太设计
Souvenirs, Antiques

☎ 5403 3551; 207 Fumin Rd; 富民路207号; ⏲ 10am-7pm; Ⓜ Changshu Rd or Jing'an Temple

The seamless transition from revolutionary terror to chic mantelpiece ornament took place with hardly a wobble. Bag Mao's bust, a repro revolutionary tin mug, Cultural Revolution prints or vintage clothing.

🏠 SIMPLY LIFE 逸居生活
Home Decor

☎ 3406 0509; 9 Dongping Rd; 东平路9号; ⏲ 10.30am-10pm; Ⓜ Changshu Rd

Fish for funky household knick-knacks, whizz-bang ceramics,

modern China designs and life-style accoutrements at this outlet; sibling branch in Xintiandi.

🏠 SKYLIGHT 天籁 *Handicrafts*

☎ 6473 5610; 28 W Fuxing Rd; 复兴西路28号; ⏲ 9.30am-9pm; Ⓜ Changshu Rd

Sneak into this incense-perfumed nook for its delicious haul of Tibetan handmade soap, silks, ethnic jewellery, devotional objects, antiques, furniture and ethnic swimwear.

🏠 SPIN 旋 *Ceramics*

☎ 6279 2545; Bldg 3, 758 Julu Rd; 巨鹿路758号3号楼; ⏲ 11am-9.30pm; Ⓜ Changshu Rd or Jing'an Temple

New-wave, zesty Jingdezhen ceramics are presented in a crisp and trendy space. Reach for fresh, invigorating pieces with cool celadon tones or square teapots and nifty half-glazed tea sets.

🏠 URBAN TRIBE 城市山民
Fashion

☎ 6433 5366; 133 W Fuxing Rd; 复兴西路133号; ⏲ 10am-10pm; Ⓜ Shanghai Library

This eco-conscious Shanghai label draws inspiration from the ethnic groups of Southeast Asia. Urban Tribe's collection of loose-fitting blouses, pants and jackets are made of natural fabrics; it also designs attractive silver jewellery.

🍴 EAT

🍴 AZUL/VIVA/VARGAS GRILL
Fusion YYY
☎ 6433 1172; 18 Dongping Rd; 东平路
18号; ⏰ 11am-11pm; Ⓜ Changshu Rd
Shanghai restaurateur Eduardo
Vargas' first venture – the hip Azul/
Viva – is arguably his best, particularly with the addition of the
3rd-floor Vargas Grill (dinner only)
in 2009. Expect Latin-style tapas
(Peruvian beef, sesame prawns)
and high-quality grilling action.

🍴 BAI'S RESTAURANT
白家餐室 *Shanghainese* Y
☎ 6437 6915; No 12, Lane 189, Wanping
Rd; 宛平路189弄12号; ⏰ 11am-2pm
& 5-10pm; Ⓜ Hengshan Rd or Zhaojiabang Rd
This family-run restaurant has only
a handful of tables and the food is
deservedly popular, so book ahead.
Try a few of Bai's fried savoury pork
ribs and tiger-skin chillies.

🍴 BAOLUO JIULOU 保罗酒楼
Shanghainese YY
☎ 6279 2827; 271 Fumin Rd; 富
民路271号; ⏰ 10.30am-4.30am;
Ⓜ Changshu Rd or Jing'an Temple
The scorching popularity of this
unpretentious venue is a sure sign
of good cookin', with much-
cherished Shanghai favourites
such as lemon-drizzled eel and
lion's head meatballs. There's no
English sign. Reserve ahead.

🍴 GINGER *Cafe* YY
☎ 6433 9437; 299 W Fuxing Rd; 复兴西
路299号; ⏰ 9am-11pm; Ⓜ Shanghai
Library; 🛜 Ⓥ
Impeccably tucked away at the
end of Le Passage, Ginger guar-
antees on-the-spot release from
Shanghai's urban turmoil. Enjoy
light meals (Asian, French and
veggie options), coffee and tea.
There are also two branches in the
Taikang Road Art Centre.

🍴 HAIKU 隐泉之语
Japanese YYY
☎ 6445 0021; 28B Taojiang Rd; 桃江路
28号乙; ⏰ 11.30am-2pm & 5.30-10pm;
Ⓜ Changshu Rd
The wackiest maki rolls in town:
try out the Ninja (shrimp, crab and
a killer spicy sauce), the Clayton
(shiitake mushrooms, snow crab
and scorched white tuna), the
Sweepee (sweet potatoes, avo-
cado and sesame seeds)
or, for the indecisive, Pimp My
Roll (everything). Book ahead.

🍴 JISHI JIULOU 吉士酒楼
Shanghainese YYY
☎ 6282 9260; 41 Tianping Rd; 天平
路41号; ⏰ 11am-2.30pm & 5-10pm;
Ⓜ Jiatong University
For Shanghainese home cooking
at its best, try out this jam-packed
restaurant. Popular choices include
crab dumplings, Grandma's braised
pork, and plenty of fish, drunken
shrimp and eel. This is the original;

branches around town go by the name Xinjishi (新吉士). Reserve.

🍴 LOST HEAVEN 花马天堂
Yunnanese YYY

☎ 6433 5126; 38 Gaoyou Rd; 高邮路 38号; ⏰ 11.30am-1.30pm & 5.30-10pm; Ⓜ Shanghai Library

Enlighten your tastebuds with the Dai and Miao folk cuisine from China's remote and ethnically infused southwest. Ease into a Yunnan chicken salad with chilli and sesame, Yunnan vegetable cakes or the Dai tribe chicken with seven spices. Book ahead.

🍴 NOODLE BULL 狠牛面
Noodles Y

☎ 6170 1299; Unit 3b, 291 Fumin Rd (entrance on Changle Rd); 富民路291号 1F3B室; Ⓜ Changshu Rd or S Shanxi Rd; Ⓥ

Far cooler than your average street-corner noodle stand (minimalist concrete chic and funky bowls), MSG-free Noodle Bull is also flat-out delicious. It doesn't matter whether you go vegetarian or for the roasted beef noodles, it's hard not to find satisfaction.

🍴 PINCHUAN 品川
Sichuanese YYY

☎ 6437 9361; 47 Taojiang Rd; 桃江 路47号; ⏰ 11am-2pm & 5-11pm; Ⓜ Changshu Rd

Even though Pinchuan has hit the upscale button repeatedly in the

past few years, this revamped villa is still a fine place to experience the peculiar tongue-tingling sensation of Sichuan cuisine. Try the sliced beef in spicy sauce, baked spare ribs with peanuts, or spicy chicken. Book ahead.

🍴 SICHUAN CITIZEN
龙门阵茶屋 *Sichuanese* Y

☎ 5404 1235; 30 Donghu Rd; 东湖路 30号; Ⓜ Changshu Rd or S Shanxi Rd

The food at the rustically chic Citizen is prepared by a busy Sichuan kitchen crew to ensure no Shanghai sweetness creeps into the peppercorn onslaught. If you're new to Sichuanese, this is a great place to try classics such as twice-cooked pork and kung pao shrimp.

🍸 DRINK

🍸 ABBEY ROAD 艾比之路 *Bar*

☎ 6431 6787; 45 Yueyang Rd; 岳阳路 45号; ⏰ 4pm-late Mon-Fri, 8.30am-late Sat & Sun; Ⓜ Changshu Rd; 🛜

Once the weather gets nice, the tree-shaded patio adds the final ingredient to make this cheap beer and classic-rock combination an irresistible favourite.

🍸 BOONNA CAFÉ 布那咖啡
Cafe

☎ 5404 6676; www.boonnacafe.com; 88 Xinle Rd; 新乐路88号; ⏰ 8am-1am; Ⓜ S Shanxi Rd; 🛜

Relaxed and snug boho cafe that boasts some of Shanghai's

cheapest coffees and smoothies, a book exchange, cool music and a solitary online terminal.

▼ BOXING CAT BREWERY
拳击猫啤酒屋 *Bar*

☎ 6431 2091; 82 W Fuxing Rd; 复兴西路82号; ⏰ 5pm-2am Mon-Fri, 11am-2am Sat & Sun; Ⓜ Shanghai Library or Changshu Rd; 📶

Popular three-floor microbrewery combining a rotating line-up of fresh beers with first-rate sandwiches and gumbo.

▼ COTTON'S 棉花酒吧 *Bar*

☎ 6433 7995; 132 Anting Rd; 安亭路132号; ⏰ 11am-2am; Ⓜ Hengshan Rd; 📶

Cotton's French Concession concept – an evocative 1930s villa, restful garden and gorgeous interior – sets the standard for Shanghai's bars.

▼ LITTLE FACE *Bar*

☎ 6466 4328; 2nd fl, 30 Donghu Rd; 东湖路30号2楼; ⏰ 5.30pm-1am; Ⓜ Changshu Rd or S Shanxi Rd

Little Face has the same antique-strewn elegance as its previous incarnation of two separate restaurants, minus the garden. It's a stylish place for pre- or post-dinner drinks, and the old opium bed has made the trip adding to the decadent undertow.

▼ LOGO *Bar*

☎ 6281 5646; 13 Xingfu Rd; 幸福路13号; ⏰ 6pm-late; Ⓜ Jiaotong University

You *could* sit down with a Pink Lady on the cigarette-burned sofas here, but this is more a place to neck a Tiger. One of the few alternative dives in town, LOgO's low-key appeal has a large following.

▼ VELVET LOUNGE *Bar*

☎ 5403 2976; 913 Julu Rd; 巨鹿路913号; ⏰ 5pm-3am Sun-Thu, to 5am Fri & Sat; Ⓜ Changshu Rd or Jing'an Temple

An anomaly among the girlie bars of Julu Rd, Velvet Lounge is a hip nightspot that has become a cult favourite among the all-night crowd.

▼ ZAPATA'S *Bar, Club*

☎ 6474 6166; 5 Hengshan Rd; 衡山路5号; ⏰ 5.30pm-2am; Ⓜ Changshu Rd; 📶

A Shanghai institution. By the time 11pm rolls around at Zapata's, folks have usually had enough margaritas that they're ready to leave the dance floor behind and start shaking it all on top of the bar.

⭐ PLAY

▢ COTTON CLUB
棉花俱乐部 *Jazz*

☎ 6437 7110; 8 W Fuxing Rd; 复兴西路8号; ⏰ 7.30pm-2am Tue-Sun; Ⓜ Changshu Rd

In a space decked out in wood and brass, the longstanding Cotton Club's house band serves up live jazz and blues to a loyal crowd.

⭐ DRAGON CLUB Club
☎ 6433 2187; 156 Fenyang Rd; 汾阳路156号; ⏱ 10pm-4am Wed & Thu, to dawn Fri & Sat; Ⓜ Changshu Rd
After-hours hangout with stylish villa ambience plus cool clientele; a favourite with moneyed Shanghainese and the late-night clubbing crowd.

⭐ JZ CLUB Jazz
☎ 6385 0269; 46 W Fuxing Rd; 复兴西路46号; ⏱ 9pm-2am; Ⓜ Changshu Rd
This is a clued-up setting where contemporary jazz, Latin and R&B is enjoyed by an enthusiastic following.

⭐ SHANGHAI FANTASIA
梦上海 Acrobatics
☎ 6248 2340; Children's Art Theatre, 643 Huashan Rd; 华山路643号儿童艺术剧院; Ⓜ Changshu Rd
The newest acrobatics show to hit Shanghai, with daily performances at 7.30pm. Call for tickets or order online through www.smartshanghai.com.

⭐ SHELTER Club
☎ 6437 0400; 5 Yongfu Rd; 永福路5号; ⏱ 9pm-4am Wed-Sun; Ⓜ Shanghai Library
The darling of the underground crowd, this reconverted bomb shelter is the city's best spot for serious music (cutting-edge DJs and hip-hop artists) and cheap drinks.

>JING'AN

Cutting a hefty swath north of the French Concession ranges the vibrant commercial district of Jing'an. A popular shopping, drinking and residential zone, the area is defined by the pulsing throb of West Nanjing Rd (named Bubbling Well Rd in Concession times), itself anchored by prestigious shopping malls and the rock-solid Shanghai Centre. Away from the commercial buzz and off the main drag, the district is charmingly detailed with pleasant *lilong* (alleyways; see also p20) with dignity and character supplied by a profusion of period architecture. Art lovers can forage north to M50, Buddhists (and the plain curious) will make a beeline for the Jade Buddha Temple, while foodies will have their hands full trying to decide where to eat. Among monuments recalling early, moneyed Jewish arrivals from Baghdad to Bombay are places such as the Shanghai Children's Palace. A burst of new nightlife venues hint at bigger things to come.

JING'AN

🔵 SEE
Former Residence of
  Mao Zedong 1 G5
Jade Buddha Temple 2 D2
Jing'an Temple 3 D5
M50 .... 4 E1
Shanghai Children's
  Palace 5 D6

🏠 SHOP
Amy Lin's Pearls &
  Jewellery .... (see 6)
Art Deco .... (see 4)

Fenshine Fashion &
  Accessories Plaza 6 H4

🍴 EAT
Bali Laguna 7 D6
Fu 1039 .... 8 B6
Lynn 9 E5
Qimin Organic Hotpot .. 10 E4
Vegetarian Lifestyle 11 F4

🍸 DRINK
Big Bamboo 12 E5
Café 85°C 13 F4

Wagas 14 F5

⭐ PLAY
Bandu Cabin .... (see 4)
Image Tunnel .... (see 4)
Muse 15 D3
Paramount Ballroom 16 D5
Shanghai Centre
  Theatre 17 E5
Sin Lounge 18 G5

Please see over for map

👁 SEE

👁 FORMER RESIDENCE OF MAO ZEDONG 毛泽东旧居

5-9, 120 N Maoming Rd; 茂名北路 **120 弄5-9 号; admission Y5;** ⏰ **9-11am & 1-4.30pm Tue-Sun;** Ⓜ **W Nanjing Rd**
Admirers of communist memorabilia will want to pop in to see the Chairman's bedroom, but the highlight is the building itself, a beautiful example of *shikumen* (stone-gate house) architecture.

👁 JADE BUDDHA TEMPLE 玉佛寺

Cnr Anyuan Rd & Jiangning Rd; 安远 路、江宁路交叉口; **admission Y20;** ⏰ **8am-4.30pm;** Ⓜ **Changshou Rd or Shanghai Train Station then taxi**
Despite swelling visitor numbers, Shanghai's most famous Buddhist temple (see also p24), named after its gorgeous effigy of the historical Buddha, maintains its sacred charm.

👁 JING'AN TEMPLE 静安寺

1686-1688 W Nanjing Rd; 南京西 路1686-1688 号; **admission Y20;** ⏰ **7.30am-5pm;** Ⓜ **Jing'an Temple**
A skyscraper needs only a few years to go up in Shanghai, but rebuilding this temple seems an eternal work in progress. The recent add-ons are eye-catching, but the main temple hall has yet to be reincarnated from a concrete

Jade Buddha Temple

bunker. The temple manages to somehow sum up Shanghai: 5% traditional, 95% rebuild.

👁 M50创意产业集聚区

50 Moganshan Rd; 莫干山路50号; Ⓜ **Shanghai Train Station**
Standout contemporary art galleries (see also p21), housed in a complex of industrial buildings down dusty Moganshan Rd. The top-notch and provocative island6 focuses on collaborative works created in a studio behind the gallery. Other notable galleries include Art Scene and twocities, the latter of which specialises in 3-D art.

Grid References

1 N Zhongshan Rd 中山北路
Zhenping Rd 镇坪路

A

B
N Zhongshan Rd 中山北路

Yichang Rd 宜昌路
N Shaanxi Rd
Aomen Rd 澳门路
Putuo Rd

Xikang Rd 西康路
Aomen Rd

Changde Rd 常德路
Changshou Rd 长寿路

2
Changshou Rd 长寿路站

Xinhui Rd
Anyuan Rd 安远路
N Shaanx

C
Aomen Rd 澳门路

Jiangning Rd 江宁路

D
Aomen Rd 澳门路

Zhijiang Dream Factory
Yuyao Rd 余姚路

3
W Guangfu Rd

JING'AN

Changping Rd 昌平路
Changping Rd 昌平路站

Yanping Rd

Kangding Rd 康定路
Changde Rd 常德路

Yuyao Rd 余姚路
Kangding Rd 康定路

4
Wanhangdu Rd 万航渡路

S Wuning Rd 武宁南路

Wuding Rd 武定路
Jiaozhou Rd 胶州路

W Wuding Rd
Wanhangdu Rd 万航渡路

5
Air Term

Bubbling Well Lane
Xuandong Internet Café
W Nanjing Rd

Tourist Information & Service Centre

Yuyao Rd 愚园路
611 Yuyuan Rd

6
See French Concession West Map p73

Jiangsu Rd 江苏路站

0   500 m
0   0.25 miles

E F G H

See Hongkou & North Shanghai Map p105

ZHABEI

C4 Moganshan Rd 莫干山路四

Ajiseh

Shanghai Railway Station 上海火车站
M 上海火车站

Shanghai Train Station 上海火车站

Train Ticket Booking Office

Bus to Pudong Airport

W Tianmu Rd 天目西路

Wusong River (Suzhou Creek)

Chang'an Rd 长安路

Yutong Rd 裕通路

Minli Rd

Hanzhong Rd 汉中路

Hengtong Rd

Gonghexin Rd

Haining Rd 海宁路

Wuchang Rd 武昌路

Jinyuan Rd

Datong Rd 大统路

Haifang Rd 海防路

Hengfeng Rd Bus Station

Hengfeng Rd 恒丰路

Hengfeng Rd

Changping Rd 昌平路

Moganshan Rd

Jiangning Rd 江宁路

Guangfu Rd 光复路

Hanzhong Rd 汉中路站

Datian Rd 大田路

Wusong River (Suzhou Creek)

Xinzha Rd 新闸路 M

Xinzha Rd 新闸路站

See The Bund & People's Square Map pp40–1

S Suzhou Rd 南苏州路

Wuding Rd 武定路

Shanhaiguan Rd 山海关路

W Beijing Rd 北京西路

Hanghe Rd

Xikang Rd 西康路

Xinzha Rd 新闸路

Shimen No 2 Rd 石门二路

Fengyang Rd 凤阳路

Xincheng Rd

N Chengdu Rd 成都北路

Tomorrow Square 明天广场

Ohel Rachel Synagogue (former)

10

13

W Beijing Rd 北京西路

Fengxian Rd

11

Westgate Mall

Taixing Rd

Wujiang Rd 吴江路

Qinghai Rd 青海路

W Nanjing Rd

Sanjiao Rd

Wusheng Rd 武胜路

Jiangyin Rd

Fengxian Rd

W Nanjing Rd 南京西路站

Shimen No 1 Rd 石门一路

12

Tongren Rd 铜仁路

Nanyang Rd

9

Post Office

17

Shanghai Centre

14

N Maoming Rd 南京西路

Bubbling Well Road Apartments

Weihai Rd 威海路

18

Dagu Rd 大沽路

Frangipani

Dagu Rd

Guangchang Park 广场公园

Shanghai Exhibition Centre

S Shaanxi Rd 陕西南路

N Shaanxi Rd 陕西北路

S Maoming Rd 茂名南路

Ruijin No 1 Rd 瑞金一路

N Chengdu Rd 成都北路

JING'AN

Fumin Rd 富民路

Middle Yan'an Rd 延安中路

See French Concession East Map pp64–5

S Shaanxi Rd 陕西南路

Changle Rd 长乐路

Jinjiang Tower

Julu Rd 巨鹿路

Okura Garden Hotel Shanghai

Middle Huaihai Rd 淮海中路

SHANGHAI'S COMMUNIST VESTIGES

In its bid to totally refashion itself as a global financial centre, Shanghai is deeply at odds with its communist heritage. But lest we forget, the city played a decisive role in China's communist history. China's communist destiny was first forged at the Site of the 1st National Congress of the CCP (p63), before the revolution shifted from factory workers to the peasants, and the Gang of Four, who controlled the latter stages of the Cultural Revolution – take a look at the rubbed-out revolutionary slogan (see the boxed text, p10) on Suzhou Creek – were based in Shanghai. Other sights include the Former Residence of Mao Zedong (p83) and the Propaganda Poster Art Centre (p74).

◎ SHANGHAI CHILDREN'S PALACE 少年宫

1799 W Nanjing Rd; 南京西路1799号; admission Y20; ⏰ 8am-6pm Wed-Sun; Ⓜ Jing'an Temple

A striking white, two-storey 1920s building, this was formerly Kadoorie House, named after its wealthy Jewish owner. Architecture detectives can still peek in the rooms of Elly Kadoorie's 1920s mansion, once the site of Shanghai's most extravagant balls. It now hosts after-school activities for kids.

🛍 SHOP

☐ AMY LIN'S PEARLS & JEWELLERY 艾敏林氏珍珠 *Pearls*

☎ 5228 2372; Room 30, 3rd fl, Fenshine Fashion & Accessories Plaza, 580 W Nanjing Rd; 南京西路580号3楼30号; ⏰ 10am-8pm; Ⓜ W Nanjing Rd

Oft-visited by dignitaries, Amy Lin's stocks high-quality lustrous salt- and fresh-water pearls of all colours, overseen by English-speaking staff who can string them into a choker or a matinée necklace.

☐ ART DECO 凹凸家具库 *Antiques*

☎ 6277 8927; Bldg 7, 50 Moganshan Rd; 莫干山路50号7号楼; ⏰ 10am-7pm

You've seen the deco buildings, now peruse the woodwork. This elegant shop, one of several retailers in the M50 complex (p83), sells stunning furniture from the city's creative heyday. Chairs start at around Y1200.

☐ FENSHINE FASHION & ACCESSORIES PLAZA 凤翔服饰礼品广场 *Fashion*

580 W Nanjing Rd; 南京西路580号; ⏰ 9am-9pm; Ⓜ W Nanjing Rd

This unassuming building is a good spot for discount purchases, with hundreds of stalls spread across two floors. Scavenge for shoes, suitcases, sunglasses, shirts, ties and electronics. Amy Lin's

Pearls (opposite) is also located here. Bargain hard.

EAT

BALI LAGUNA 巴厘岛
Indonesian YYY
☎ 6248 6970; 1649 W Nanjing Rd; 南京西路1649号; ⏰ 11am-10.30pm; Ⓜ Jing'an Temple

This Indonesian restaurant has an open longhouse interior with a tranquil lakeside setting in Jing'an Park. Waiters in sarongs serve up excellent dishes, such as seafood curry in a fresh pineapple, gado gado (vegetable salad with peanut sauce) and *kalio daging* (beef in coconut milk, lemongrass and curry sauce). Reserve a table or stop by for a drink on the terrace.

FU 1039 福一零三九
Shanghainese YYY
☎ 6288 1179; 1039 Yuyuan Rd; 愚园路1039号; ⏰ 11am-2.30pm & 5-11pm; Ⓜ Jiangsu Rd

Set in a three-storey 1913 villa, Fu attains an old-fashioned charm uncommon in design-driven Shanghai. The succulent smoked fish starter and stewed pork in soy sauce are recommended, with the sweet-and-sour Mandarin fish coming in close behind. The entrance, down an alley and on the left, is unmarked. Little English is spoken.

Enjoy Indonesian cuisine by the lake at Bali Laguna

Ⅲ LYNN 琳怡
Shanghainese YYY

☎ 6247 0101; 99-1 Xikang Rd; 西康路
99-1号; ⓧ 11.30am-10.30pm; Ⓜ W
Nanjing Rd

Newfangled dim sum and Shang-
hai-meets-Cantonese cuisine
in a splendidly stylish setting.
Adventurous standouts mix with
traditional dishes: look for eggplant with minced pork, chicken
with sesame pockets and deep-
fried ribs with honey and garlic.
Sundays bring an all-you-can-eat
brunch for Y78. Reserve a table.

ⅢQIMIN ORGANIC HOTPOT
齐民有机中国火锅 *Hotpot* YYY

☎ 6258 8777; 407 N Shaanxi Rd; 陕西
北路407号; ⓧ 11am-2pm & 5-9pm;
Ⓜ W Nanjing Rd; Ⓥ

Qimin makes use of a 6th-century
treatise on agriculture and food

MOBILE COMMUNICATION

Wherever you go in Shanghai, pack
a mobile. Spoken English is scarce, so
don't expect to be understood, even if
you speak slowly and loudly. From talk-
ing to taxi drivers to buying train tickets
or emergencies, have a local contact in
Shanghai on speed dial so you can phone
to do the business for you. A particularly
useful number to have is the **Shanghai
Call Centre** (☎ 962 288): it's a free
24-hour English-language hot line that
can answer cultural, entertainment or
transport enquiries.

---

preparation to prepare healthy,
sophisticated hotpots for discern-
ing diners.

ⅢVEGETARIAN LIFESTYLE
枣子树 *Chinese, Vegetarian* YY

☎ 6215 7566; 258 Fengxian Rd; 奉贤
路258号; ⓧ 11am-9pm; Ⓜ W Nanjing
Rd; Ⓥ

The Chinese sign on the door says
it all: 'No smoking, no alcohol,
no eggs and no meat'. The food
here is simply delectable, and the
health-conscious ecofriendly men-
tality extends all the way to the
toothpicks (made from cornflour).

Ⓨ DRINK

Ⓨ BIG BAMBOO *Bar*

☎ 6256 2265; 132 Nanyang Rd; 南阳
路132号; ⓧ 11am-2am; Ⓜ Jing'an
Temple; 🛜

This is a huge, extroverted sports
bar ranging over two floors with a
mammoth sports screen backed
up by a constellation of TV sets,
Guinness, pool and darts.

Ⓨ CAFÉ 85°C 85度C咖啡店
Cafe

408 N Shaanxi Rd; 陕西北路408号;
ⓧ 24hr; Ⓜ W Nanjing Rd

This Taiwanese chain serves good-
quality, inexpensive coffee and
tea, but it's particularly notable
for its bizarre pastries (often
savoury, not sweet), if you're
ready to experience a modern-

Han Yuqi

A local artist and university professor, Han founded Image Tunnel (p90) in 2005.

What's your opinion of Shanghai? You might think that it has a lot of drawbacks – no peace and quiet – but there are many opportunities here. Many young people come to M50 to work on projects, so for me it is really an exciting place. **Your favourite Shanghai film?** There are a lot of Shanghainese who have never seen old Shanghai movies. In 2005, I showed some silent films and was afraid that everyone would get bored. But afterwards everyone said, 'Wow, that Ruan Lingyu [famous 1930s actress] is really amazing!' **If you could change one thing...** The Chinese attitude towards art. Most Chinese don't think of spending money on art. Our tradition has always been: save, save, save; don't spend money on unnecessary things. But young Chinese are different.

LILONG 里弄

Jing'an has a lovely collection of old alleyways. Delve down **Bubbling Well Lane** (Map pp84–5, B6; 395 Yuyuan Rd; 愚园路395号) or **611 Yuyuan Rd** (Map pp84–5, B6; 611 Yuyuan Rd; 愚园路611号), both near the Jiangsu Rd metro, and hunt down **Bubbling Well Road Apartments** (Map pp84–5, E5; Lane 1025, W Nanjing Rd; 南京西路1025弄), which has rows of new-style lilong (alleyway) houses built between 1928 and 1932.

day Chinese breakfast on the go. There are branches throughout Shanghai.

☑ WAGAS 沃歌斯 Cafe

☎ 5292 5228; Bldg 11a, Citic Sq, 1168 W Nanjing Rd; 南京西路1168号下一层 11a室; ⏱ 7am-9.30pm; Ⓜ W Nanjing Rd; 📶

A dependable local cafe that's good for coffee and Western breakfast. Locations throughout Shanghai.

⭐ PLAY

⭐ BANDU CABIN 半度音乐 Live Music

☎ 6276 8267; www.bandumusic.com; Bldg 11, 50 Moganshan Rd; 莫干山路 50号11楼; ⏱ 10am-6.30pm Sun-Fri, 10am-10pm Sat; Ⓜ Shanghai Train Station

Phone up after 10am on Friday and book a seat for the traditional Chinese music performances every Saturday at 8pm at this cafe in the M50 complex (p83).

⭐ IMAGE TUNNEL 影像隧道 Cinema

☎ 2813 0548; www.imagetunnel.com; 2nd fl, Bldg 19, 50 Moganshan Rd; 莫干 山路50号19号楼2楼; ⏱ 7pm Sat; Ⓜ Shanghai Train Station

This small gallery screens independent Chinese films on Saturdays (among other projects), though English subtitles are not guaranteed.

⭐ MUSE Club

☎ 5213 5228; www.museshanghai .cn; New Factories, 68 Yuyao Rd; 余姚 路68号同乐坊; ⏱ 8.30pm-4.30am; Ⓜ Changping Rd

One of the city's hottest clubs, Muse boasts two floors, with house music downstairs and hip-hop upstairs. Don't bother looking for a large dance floor; just squeeze into the crowd or jump up on a private table (Y3000 per night).

⭐ PARAMOUNT BALLROOM 百乐门 Ballroom Dancing

☎ 6249 8866; 218 Yuyuan Rd; 豫园路 218号; ⏱ 1pm-12.30am; Ⓜ Jing'an Temple

This old art-deco theatre was the biggest nightclub in Shanghai in the 1930s before transforming into the Red Capital Cinema in the Mao years. An unusual throwback in today's Shanghai, it has low-key tea dances in the afternoon as well as ballroom dancing in the evening. Dance partners are Y35 to Y45 for 10 minutes.

⭐ SHANGHAI CENTRE THEATRE
上海商城剧院 *Acrobatics*
☎ 6279 8948; www.shanghaicentre .com; 1376 W Nanjing Rd; 南京西路 1376号; Ⓜ Jing'an Temple
With joint-popping performances at 7.30pm most nights, this is one of the main venues in town for acrobatics. Routines from the Shanghai Acrobatics Troupe (tickets Y100 to Y280) rotate nightly, but don't attempt them at home.

⭐ SIN LOUNGE *Club*
☎ 6267 7779; 23rd fl, Want Want Bldg, 211 Shimen No 1 Rd; 石门一路211号 旺旺大厦23楼; ⏱ 9pm-2am Sun-Thu, 9pm-5am Fri & Sat; Ⓜ W Nanjing Rd
Cool views, slick design and a large dance space are the temptations in this glamorous hotspot. Big-names regularly man the turntables here; colossal floor-to-ceiling windows serve up late-night Shanghai as the dance-floor backdrop.

>PUDONG

Pudong is one of those Chinese place names that most Westerners know well before setting foot in Shanghai. More than one-and-a-half times bigger than urban Shanghai itself, Pudong was a flatland of boggy farms in 1990; further back in time, it was home to the godowns (warehouses) and compradors (buyers) of Shanghai's foreign trading companies. Today the only things sprouting out of the ground are skyscrapers, and Pudong has become Shanghai's and China's economic powerhouse. The high-rise area directly across from the Bund is the Lujiazui Finance and Trade Zone, where the Shanghai Stock Exchange, China's largest stock market, is located. From the unmistakable Oriental Pearl TV Tower, the eight-lane-wide Century Ave runs over 4km to Century Park, close to where MagLevs glide swiftly into the universe of soaring highrise buildings. Next up for Pudong? You guessed it – another skyscraper. Aiming for a 2014 completion date, the 128-storey Shanghai Tower will one day dwarf the rest of Lujiazui at a towering height of 632m.

PUDONG

◎ SEE
Jinmao Tower 1 B3
Oriental Pearl TV Tower ..2 B2
Riverside Promenade 3 A3
Shanghai History
    Museum ....(see 2)

Shanghai World Financial
    Center 4 C3

🍽 EAT
On 56 ....(see 1)
South Beauty ....(see 5)
Superbrand Mall 5 B3

🍸 DRINK
100 Century Avenue ....(see 4)
Cloud 9 ....(see 1)

👁 SEE

📷 JINMAO TOWER 金茂大厦

☎ 5047 5101; 88 Century Ave; 世纪大道88号; observation deck admission adult/student Y88/60; ⏱ 8.30am-10pm; Ⓜ Lujiazui

Rising above the clouds, the splendid Jinmao stands beside the shimmering Shanghai World Financial Center like an art-deco pagoda. Shoot to the 88th-floor observation deck to put Shanghai in a splendid nutshell. Time your visit at dusk for both day and night views. Alternatively, sample the same view through the carbonated fizz of a gin and tonic at Cloud 9 (p97).

📷 ORIENTAL PEARL TV TOWER 东方明珠广播电视塔

☎ 5879 1888; admission Y100-280; ⏱ 8am-10pm; Ⓜ Lujiazui

Love it or hate it, this 468m-tall bauble-adorned tripod has become a symbol of Pudong and the Shanghai renaissance. Join the queue for high-altitude views or head to the basement to visit the highly recommended Shanghai History Museum (right).

📷 RIVERSIDE PROMENADE 滨江大道

⏱ 6.30am-11pm; Ⓜ Lujiazui

Hands down the best walk in Pudong, this promenade features sublime full-length views of the Bund in its unfurled, ornate scroll. Choicely positioned cafes and ice-cream stands look out over the water.

📷 SHANGHAI HISTORY MUSEUM 上海城市历史发展陈列馆

☎ 5879 8888; Oriental Pearl TV Tower basement; 东方明珠塔; admission Y35; ⏱ 8am-9.30pm; Ⓜ Lujiazui

One of Shanghai's top sights, this fun museum charts the city's highs and lows from its days as a cotton-producing town to its grandiose, opium-wreathed heyday and beyond. Life-size models of traditional shops are staffed by realistic waxworks and some exhibits are hands-on or accompanied by creative video presentations.

📷 SHANGHAI WORLD FINANCIAL CENTER 上海环球金融中心

☎ 5878 0101; 100 Century Ave; 世纪大道100号; observation deck 94th/97th/100th fl, adult Y100/110/150, under 18 yr Y70/80/100; ⏱ 8am-11pm (last entry 10pm); Ⓜ Lujiazui

Completed in 2008, China's tallest building (492m) is also the world's third tallest (for now). Don't feel short-changed by the bronze medal though – the observation decks, located at the bottom and top of the trapezoidal hole, are still the world's highest. If queues are long, head up to the building's

He Nong

*Originally from Jiangxi province, He Nong moved to Shanghai in 1992 to
[stu]d law school. He is now the managing partner of a Pudong law firm.*

[What] do you think about Shanghai? Other places in China are more relaxed –
[you sp]end less time working and more time living – but in Shanghai it's the
[oppo]site! **What do you think about copyright law in China? There are a lot
[of pir]ated goods here. Will that change?** It will certainly change, but not over-
[night.] Piracy is linked to economic development. After people's living standards
[impro]ve, they might not turn to pirating goods anymore. And perhaps the
[gover]nment will be harsher. **Do international companies ever contact you
[about] copyright infringement?** There are a lot of companies who contact us
[about] this, but because it is complicated, the legal fees are high. So then they
[have] to decide: is it worth it for us to spend so much money?

91st-floor restaurant-bar 100 Century Avenue (right) instead.

⬛ ZENDAI MUSEUM OF MODERN ART 证大现代艺术馆
☎ 5033 9801; No 28, Lane 199, Fangdian Rd; 芳甸路199弄28号; admission Y20, free Wed; ⏰ 10am-6pm Tue & Thu-Sun, 10am-9pm Wed; Ⓜ Science & Technology Museum

Fine museum with an emphasis on contemporary exhibitions in a modern art space.

🛍 SHOP

AP XINYANG FASHION & GIFTS MARKET 亚太新阳服饰礼品市场 Fashion, Souvenirs
⏰ 10am-8pm; Ⓜ Science & Technology Museum

One-stop shopping in all its bargain-basement glory is found in the Science & Technology Museum metro station. There's an entire fabric market here (for tailored clothing), rows upon rows of pearls, plus all the usual suspects: shoes, sports equipment, T-shirts, electronics… Bargain hard.

🍴 EAT

🍴 ON 56 意庐 Diverse YYY
☎ 5047 1234; 54th-56th fl, Grand Hyatt, Jinmao Tower, 88 Century Ave; 世纪大道88号君悦大酒店54-56层; ⏰ 11.30am-2.30pm & 5.30-10.30pm; Ⓜ Lujiazui

The Grand Hyatt in the Jinmao Tower offers a constellation of high-altitude restaurants (Cantonese, Japanese, Italian and buffet), all of which come with superb vistas looking out into the void. Don't forget to reserve a table.

🍴 SOUTH BEAUTY 俏江南
Sichuanese YYY
☎ 5047 1817; 10th fl, Superbrand Mall, 168 W Lujiazui Rd; 陆家嘴西路168号10楼; ⏰ 11am-10pm; Ⓜ Lujiazui

The stuffed chillies at the entrance hint at what's to come, but for those who enjoy milder tastes, southern dishes will soothe the tastebuds. You'll need to reserve for the coveted Bund-facing window seats. Branches throughout Shanghai.

🍴 SUPERBRAND MALL 正大广场 Diverse Y–YYY
168 W Lujiazui Rd; 陆家嘴西路168号; ⏰ 10am-10pm; Ⓜ Lujiazui

This gargantuan, central mall has floors upon floors of restaurants, such as South Beauty (above), to cater to all tastes and budgets.

🍸 DRINK

🍸 100 CENTURY AVENUE Bar
☎ 3855 1428; 91st-92nd fl, Park Hyatt, Shanghai World Financial Center, 100 Century Ave; 世纪大道100号柏悦酒店91-92楼; ⏰ 4.30pm-1am Mon-Sat, 4.30-10.30pm Sun; Ⓜ Lujiazui

Head up to 100 Century Avenue for a real Shang high. There's a downstairs restaurant area (with six open kitchens) and upstairs drinking area (not against the windows). Access is through the Park Hyatt.

☖ CLOUD 9 九重天酒廊 *Bar*
☎ 5049 1234; 87th fl, Jinmao Tower, 88 Century Ave; 世纪大道88号金茂大厦87楼; ⏱ 5pm-1am Mon-Fri, 11am-2am Sat & Sun; Ⓜ Lujiazui
Pudong's coolest bar, Cloud 9 is a fantastic place to watch day fade into night as the neon slowly flick-ers on across the curving horizon. Access is through the Grand Hyatt.

⭐ PLAY

⭐ ORIENTAL ART CENTER
上海东方艺术中心 *Live music*
☎ 6854 1234; www.shoac.com.cn; 425 Dingxiang Rd; 浦东丁香路425号; Ⓜ Science & Technology Museum
This futuristic venue stages all manner of concerts, including classical, jazz, dance and opera. In the past it has staged traditional Chinese music on Saturday nights – call for updates.

>XUJIAHUI & SOUTH SHANGHAI

With its sporadic Jesuit monuments, huge malls, roaring traffic and high-rise salmon-tiled residential blocks, Xujiahui succinctly sums up the city as a whole. Formerly known as Zicawei or Sicawei by Shanghai expats, Xujiahui's traffic-snarled intersection and busy roads were once a quiet Jesuit settlement with a 17th-century ancestry. Almost blotted out by hasty construction and deconstruction, some of Xujiahui's precious Catholic charms still survive among the heaving roads and anonymous architecture. Most locals are here for convenient one-stop shopping at Grand Gateway and other outsize malls. With patience and a keen eye for the historic, visitors can still wander the district, unearthing its Jesuit heritage. Rising in South Shanghai are the ancient Longhua Temple and its pagoda.

XUJIAHUI & SOUTH SHANGHAI

☾ SEE
Bibliotheca Zi-Ka-Wei ...1 B2
Longhua Pagoda 2 D5
Longhua Temple 3 D5
St Ignatius Cathedral 4 B2

☐ SHOP
Grand Gateway 5 B2
Liuligongfang ....(see 5)

☗ EAT
Donglaishun 6 B1
Uighur Restaurant 7 A2
Ye Olde Station
    Restaurant 8 B2

W Huaihai Rd 淮海西路

Huashan 华山路

Guangyuan Rd 元路

Zhaojiabang Rd 肇家浜路站

Dong'an Rd 东安路

Guangyuan Rd 广元路

W Guangyuan Rd 汇西路

International Peace Maternity Hospital

Xujiahui Park 徐家汇公园

Hengshan Rd 衡山路

Zhaojiabang Rd 肇嘉浜路

Pacific Department Store

5

Hongqiao Rd 虹桥路

Kuhong Rd

Xujiahui 徐家汇站

Bus to Pudong Airport

Metro City

XUHUI

S Wanping Rd 宛平南路

Yishan Rd 宜山路

Nandan Rd 南丹路

Guangqi Park

4 1 Puxi Rd
Ziyang Rd 8
Jesuit
Observatory

E Nandan Rd 黄丹东路

Longhua Hospital

Puhuitang Rd 蒲汇塘路路

N Caoxi Rd

Cixun St

Tianyaoqiao Rd 天钥桥路

Xietu Rd 斜土路

Lingling Rd 零陵路

Yishan Rd 宜山路站

Wending Rd

Kaixuan Rd

Shanghai Stadium 上海体育场

W Zhongshan Rd 中山西路

Shanghai Indoor Stadium 上海体育馆

Shanghai Indoor Stadium 上海体育馆站

Shanghai Stadium

S Zhongshan No 2 Rd 中山南二路

Shanghai Swimming Pool

Shanghai Sightseeing Buses

Longhua Park 龙华公园

N Caoxi Rd

Caoxi Rd 漕溪路站

Longhua Park 龙华公园

Martyrs Memorial

W Longhua Rd 龙华西路

Tianlin Rd 田林路

3 2

Qinzhou Rd

Caoxi Park 漕溪公园

Longwu Rd

Shanghai Everbright Convention & Exhibition Centre

Caobao Rd 漕宝路站

Caobao Rd 漕宝路

Longcao Rd 龙漕路

Longcao Rd 龙漕路站

0 500 m
0 0.25 miles

◉ SEE

◉ BIBLIOTHECA ZI-KA-WEI
徐家汇藏书楼

☎ 6487 4095, ext 208; 80 N Caoxi Rd; 漕溪北路80号; admission free; ⏰ library tour 2-4pm Sat; Ⓜ Xujiahui

Of Xujiahui's prized Jesuit monuments, none is as splendid as the St Ignatius Catholic Library, built in 1847. Reserve a spot on the free 15-minute Saturday tours of the magnificent library (大书房) or peek into the old reading room (2nd floor) during the week.

◉ LONGHUA TEMPLE & PAGODA 龙华寺、龙华塔

☎ 6457 6327; 2853 Longhua Rd; 龙华路2853号; admission Y10; ⏰ 7am-4.30pm; Ⓜ Longcao Rd or 🚌 44 from Xujiahui

The saffron-coloured halls of Longhua temple make up Shang-

WORTH THE TRIP: QIBAO 七宝

Well within reach of the centre of town (8km southwest of Xujiahui), the ancient canal town of **Qibao** (2 Minzhu Rd; 闵行区民主路2号; admission Y30; ⏰ 8.30am-4.30pm; Ⓜ Qibao) dates back to the Northern Song dynasty (AD 960–1127), reaching its apogee during the Ming and Qing dynasties. Qibao is littered with traditional historic architecture, threaded by small, busy alleyways and cut by a picturesque canal. Vestiges of village handicrafts survive, including traditional wooden-bucket makers, a traditional distillery and a remarkable miniature carving museum. If you can blot out the crowds, Qibao will bring you some of the flavours of old China.

The best strategy is to just wander the streets, though the ticket office will provide you with a map marked with the nine official sights. The best of the bunch include the Cotton Textile Mill, the **Shadow Puppet Museum** (⏰ performances 1-3pm Wed & Sun), Zhou's Miniature Carving House and the Old Wine Shop (still an active distillery). Half-hour **boat rides** (per person Y10; ⏰ 8.30am-5pm) ferry passengers along the picturesque canal from Number One Bridge to Dongtangtan (东塘滩) and back. It's also worth checking out the decrepit **Catholic Church** (天主教堂; Tianzhu Jiaotang; 50 Nan St), adjacent to a convent off Nan St, south of the canal. The single-spire edifice dates back to 1867. It isn't on the official map, but you can reach it down an alley off Yutang St.

Souvenir hunters and diners will be agog at the choice of shops and eateries simply stuffed along the narrow streets. Wander along Bei Dajie, north of the canal, for a plethora of small shops in traditional two-storey dwellings selling fans, dolls, tea and wooden handicrafts. Nan Dajie is full of snacks and small eateries including No 14, which sells sweet *tang yuan* dumplings, and No 19, which is a rarely seen traditional tea house. The Old Wine Shop (21 Nan Dajie) has a quieter 2nd-floor restaurant (dishes Y10 to Y38, local wine from Y11) overlooking the street. Metro line 9 runs directly here; otherwise a taxi from the centre of Shanghai costs Y60 (but you risk getting caught in traffic).

hai's oldest and largest temple complex. It's far to the south of the city, and sees relatively few tourists. Among its halls stands one replete with glittering *luohan* (Buddhist monks who are recognised as having achieved enlightenment). The Longhua Temple Fair (p26) sees the temple at its most colourful and active. Opposite the temple rises the seven-storey Longhua Pagoda, first built in AD 977.

ST IGNATIUS CATHEDRAL
徐家汇天主堂
☎ 6438 4632; 158 Puxi Rd; 浦西路 158号; ⏱ 1-4.30pm Sat & Sun, knock at gate for admission; M Xujiahui

Its arches and spires are echoed in adjacent local architecture, all the way up to the huge tower block north of the cathedral. Just south of the church (built in 1904, and which served as a grain warehouse during the Cultural Revolution) stands the former Jesuit Observatory within the Shanghai Meteorological Bureau. The guard may stop you, but show him the Chinese characters in the heading above and he should let you into the church for a peek. Across North Caoxi Rd is the former convent of the Helpers of the Holy Souls, now Ye Olde Station Restaurant (p103).

St Ignatius Cathedral

SHOP

GRAND GATEWAY
港汇广场 *Mall*
☎ 6407 0115; 1 Hongqiao Rd; 虹桥路 1号; ⏱ 10am-10pm M Xujiahui

With its glittering twin towers rising over Xujiahui metro station, this vast mall ranges from sports in the basement, through clothing, a huge panoply of restaurants and a multiscreen cinema on the top floor.

EAT

DONGLAISHUN 东来顺

Hotpot   YY

☎ 6474 7797; 235 Guangyuan Rd;
广元路235号; ⏰ 10.30am-2am;
Ⓜ Xujiahui

Hotpot king Donglaishun enjoys a
reputation among locals as highly
burnished as its brass hotpots. Perfect for one of those clammy, frigid
Shanghai winters, but any season
will do. There's no English menu so
hand gesticulations are in order, or
point at the characters in this book
(p149). Look for the green sign
across the road from Ajisen.

UIGHUR RESTAURANT
维吾尔餐厅 *Uighur*   Y

☎ 6468 9188, 6468 9198; 80 Yishan
Rd; 宜山路80号; ⏰ 10am-2am;
Ⓜ Xujiahui

The only thing that will tear you
away from the fine lamb kebabs,
whole shoulder of lamb or *laohu
cai* (spicy tomato, cucumber and
onion salad) are the waiters dragging diners off for a quick whirl to
accompanying Uighur folk tunes.

Juicy lamb kebabs at Uighur Restaurant

NEIGHBOURHOODS

XUJIAHUI & SOUTH SHANGHAI

STAINED GLASS

The one-of-a-kind crystal art pieces at **Liuligongfang** (琉璃工房; ☎ 6407 0160; Unit 293, 2nd fl, Grand Gateway) make for a unique gift. Marvel at iridescent *pâte-de-verre* creations such as contemplative monks, compassionate bodhisattvas and exquisite earrings and pendants, all designed by a Taiwanese actress-turned-artist (who also owns TMSK, p70). Pieces are on sale from outlets in Xintiandi, Grand Gateway (p101), by People's Park on West Nanjing Rd, and various other shops around town.

🍴 YE OLDE STATION RESTAURANT 上海老站

Shanghainese   YY

☎ 6427 2233; 201 N Caoxi Rd; 漕溪北路201号; ☽ 11am-10.30pm; Ⓜ **Xujiahui**

You can't miss this oddly named restaurant when sifting through Xujiahui's Jesuit treasures. Formerly a convent, the lovely building, with its upstairs chapel intact, sits alongside other period gems (as well as two railway carriages parked out the back). The food here is not exactly pulse-raising, but the venue is unforgettable.

>HONGKOU & NORTH SHANGHAI

Crossing Waibaidu Bridge (formerly Garden Bridge) from the Bund brings you into Hongkou district, once the American Settlement, which later merged with the British Settlement to create the International Settlement. The strip along Suzhou Creek still maintains a historic dignity and precarious upward mobility. This is reflected in its splendid buildings, including the Astor House Hotel, the Post Office and other Concession-era gems. Thousands of Jewish refugees fleeing persecution in Europe sought sanctuary in Hongkou in the 1930s, bringing a distinctly Jewish flavour to parts of the district. To the west, Zhabei – once infamous for its brothels, sweatshops and slums – was flattened by the Japanese in 1932. Although the area is much grittier and more threadbare than the Bund or French Concession, it has become one of the hot new spots in Shanghai. Also referred to as the North Bund, Hongkou has had a handful of hip new hotels, restaurants and entertainment venues open in the last year, bringing the promise of more to come.

HONGKOU & NORTH SHANGHAI

◉ SEE
Duolun Road Cultural
 Street 1 C2
Hongkew Methodist
 Church 2 D4
Lu Xun Memorial Hall 3 C1
Ohel Moishe Synagogue ..4 F3

Post Museum 5 C4
Ward Road Jail 6 F3
Xiahai Buddhist
 Monastery 7 F3

🛍 SHOP
Qipu Market 8 C4

🍴 EAT
Factory 9 D3
Xindalu 10 D4

★ PLAY
Chinatown 11 C3

◉ SEE

◉ DUOLUN ROAD CULTURAL STREET 多伦文化名人街

Duolun Rd; 多伦路; **Ⓜ E Baoxing Rd**
It's sleepy, but this pleasantly restored street is a fun place to wander in low gear. Look out for the 1928 Christian Hongde Temple (鸿德堂) at No 59, sort through the clutter of Mao-era bric-a-brac at No 181, or sip some tea while catching a Chinese classic at **Old Film Café** (No 123).

◉ FISHERMAN'S WHARF 渔人码头

Yangshupu Rd; 杨树浦路; **Ⓜ Yangshu-pu Rd then taxi or ferry**
This new attraction was scheduled to open in 2010 and consists of a fishing museum and entertainment and shopping complex. It should be served by a new ferry line.

◉ HONGKEW METHODIST CHURCH 景灵堂

135 Kunshan Rd; 昆山路135号; **Ⓜ N Sichuan Rd**
Built in 1923, this church was the venue for Chiang Kaishek's marriage to Song Meiling (see p137).

◉ LU XUN MEMORIAL HALL 鲁迅纪念馆

☎ 6540 2288; Lu Xun Park, 2288 N Sichuan Rd; 四川北路2288号、鲁迅公园; **admission free;** ◷ **9am-5pm;** **Ⓜ Hongkou Football Stadium**

This modern museum presents the life and literature of Lu Xun, one of China's best-loved authors. Peruse the first editions, photographs and clothes – including a fedora and a lambskin-lined coat. Lu Xun's Shanghai home (and final residence from 1933 to 1936) is nearby at No 9, Lane 132, Shanyin Rd (山阴路132弄9号), an area of lovely *lilong* (alleyway) homes.

◉ OHEL MOISHE SYNAGOGUE 摩西会堂

☎ 6541 5008; 62 Changyang Rd; 长阳路62号; **admission Y50;** ◷ **9am-5pm;** **Ⓜ Dalian Rd,** 🚌 **33 from the Bund**

Duolun Road Cultural Street

LU XUN

Lu Xun (born Zhou Shuren; 1881–1936) is one of China's most famous writers and is often regarded as the originator of modern Chinese literature. Part of China's May 4 literary movement, his main achievement was to break from the classical literary traditions of the past – unintelligible to most Chinese – to create literature in the modern vernacular. A fierce critic of China's social ills, Lu Xun is best known for his works *A Madman's Diary* and *The True Story of Ah Q*.

This synagogue lies in the heart of the 1940s Jewish ghetto. It now houses the new Shanghai Jewish Refugees Museum, an excellent introduction to the lives of approximately 20,000 Central European refugees who fled to Shanghai to escape the Nazis.

◉ POST MUSEUM 邮政博物馆
2nd fl, 276 N Suzhou Rd; 苏州北路 276号2楼; admission free; ⏱ 9am-5pm
It may sound like a yawner, but the Post Museum is actually a pretty interesting place. Learn all about the imperial pony express, tap your foot to China's official postal hymn *(The Song of the Mail Swan Geese)* and check out the pre- and post-Liberation stamps (from 1888 to 1978). On the 5th floor is a rooftop garden with panoramic views.

⌂ SHOP

▤ QIPU MARKET
七浦服装市场 *Fashion*
168 & 183 Qipu Rd; 七浦路168 & 183号; ⏱ 5am-5pm (west side), 7am-7pm (east side); Ⓜ Tiantong Rd
Consisting of two rundown, rabbit warren–like department stores surrounding the North Henan Rd intersection, Qipu Market is one big 'everything must go now' sale. Do as the locals do and push through the hordes of people searching for pretty much any item of clothing you can think of for around Y50. Haggle hard.

HISTORICAL WALK

During WWII, Shanghai was one of the few safe havens for Jews fleeing the Holocaust in Europe because it required neither a passport nor visa to enter. The Hongkou ghetto, established by the Japanese, grew to shelter a synagogue, schools, a local paper, hospitals and enough cafes and rooftop gardens to gain the epithet 'Little Vienna'. Wander the immediate area around the Ohel Moishe Synagogue – down Zhoushan Rd, west along Huoshan Rd and north up Haimen Rd – for traces of the old Jewish presence. Also hunt down the **Xiahai Buddhist Monastery** (cnr of Haimen & Kunming Rds; admission Y5; ⏱ 7am-4pm) and the British-built **Ward Road Jail** (Zhoushan Rd).

🍴 EAT

🍴 FACTORY 意工场

Fusion YYY

☎ 6563 3393; www.factoryshanghai
.com; Bldg 4, 29 Shajing Rd; 沙泾路
29号4号楼; ⏰ 8am-midnight; Ⓜ N
Sichuan Rd or Hailun Rd; 📶 Ⓥ
Shanghai really needs more
places like this – it's fun (there's a
recording studio and art gallery
on-site), the food is delicious and
it's a promising cultural nexus. Dig
into creations such as the k-pao
chicken salad or peppercorn-crust-
ed scallops. Check the website for
events and exhibits.

🍴 XINDALU 新大陆

Chinese YYY

☎ 6393 1234, ext 6318; 1st fl, Hyatt
on the Bund, 199 Huangpu Rd; 黄浦
路199号外滩茂悦大酒店1楼;
⏰ 11.30am-2.30pm & 6-11pm; Ⓜ Tiantong Rd

Offering the city's premier roast
duck experience, this upscale
hotel restaurant pulls out all
the stops, importing necessary
ingredients direct from the capital
in order to make your Peking duck
as authentic as possible. It also
serves up fine Zhejiang cuisine,
such as beggar's chicken (order in
advance). Reserve.

⭐ PLAY

⭐ CHINATOWN 半度音乐

Cabaret

☎ 6258 2078; www.chinatownshang
hai.com; 471 Zhapu Rd; 乍浦路471号;
admission free; ⏰ 8am-2pm Wed-Sat;
Ⓜ N Sichuan Rd
The blush-inducing Chinatown
Dolls take to the stage in an old
Buddhist temple north of the
Bund. This is burlesque the way it
should be – playful, clever, pure
entertainment.

Qinghefang Old Street, Hangzhou (p110)

HANGZHOU

The dismal approach into Hangzhou by train does nothing to evoke the city's stupendous **West Lake** (西湖) and its green, well-tended environs. Hangzhou enjoyed great prosperity as capital of the Southern Song dynasty (AD 1127–1279), but was badly destroyed by Taiping rebels in the mid-19th century. Much of modern Hangzhou has consequently been rebuilt.

Originally devised in the 8th century, West Lake is crossed by the traffic-free **Su Causeway** (苏堤) and the **Bai Causeway** (白堤). The lake lacks a central must-see feature; simply wander around the lake in either direction or take a boat (Y45). Attached to the northern shore by the Bai Causeway is **Gushan Island** (孤山). The road just west of the **Mausoleum of General Yue Fei** (岳庙; Beishan Lu; 北山路; admission Y25; ☯ 7am-6pm) on the north shore leads to energetic hill walks that reach **Baopu Taoist Temple** (抱朴道院; admission Y5) and **Baochu Pagoda** (保俶塔). Rising south of West Lake, the **Leifeng Pagoda** (雷峰塔; admission Y40; ☯ 7.30am-9pm summer, 8am-5.30pm winter) is a recent rebuild.

West of the lake, lovely **Lingyin Temple** (灵隐寺; Lingyin Lu; 灵隐路; grounds & temple Y65; ☯ 7am-5pm) stands across from a collection of old Buddhist carvings on **Feilai Peak** (飞来峰), which means 'Peak flying from afar'. Among tea bushes in the hills southwest of West Lake is the **China Tea Museum** (中国茶叶博物馆; Longjing Lu; 龙井路; admission free; ☯ 8.30am-4.30pm).

East of West Lake, **Qinghefang Old Street** (清河坊历史文化街) is an entertaining take on old Hangzhou; pop into the **Chinese Medicine Museum** (中药博物馆; 95 Dajing Gang; admission Y10; ☯ 8.30am-5.30pm).

INFORMATION

Location 170km southwest of Shanghai.

Getting there Express trains leave from Shanghai South Train Station (p143; Y54, 80 minutes, 11 daily). The first train is at 7.20am; the last return train at 8.03pm. Six daily buses (Y100, three hours) go to and from Pudong airport.

Getting around Get a swipe card and use the city's bright red public-bike scheme (free first hour, Y200 deposit; ☯ kiosks open 6am-9pm Apr-Oct, 6.30am-8pm Nov-Mar).

Money Bank of China (中国银行; 177 Laodong Lu; 劳动路177号; ☯ 9am-5pm) Has a 24-hour ATM.

Sleeping Shangri-La (杭州香格里拉饭店; ☎ 8797 7951; www.shangri-la.com; 78 Beishan Lu; 北山路78号; d Y1900, with lake-view Y2500).

When to go All seasons; avoid public holidays.

Above A family day out on West Lake

SUZHOU

Suzhou is famed for its private gardens, canals and silk. Comparisons with Venice are way off the mark, but a gentle meander around its streets reveals attractive vignettes.

The tiny **Garden of the Master of the Nets** (网师园; off Shiquan Jie; 靠近十全街; off-peak/peak Y20/30; ☻ 7.30am-5.30pm), dating to the 12th century, is a gorgeous composition of halls and pavilions. The expansive **Humble Administrator's Garden** (拙政园; 178 Dongbei Jie; 东北街178号; off-peak/peak Y50/70; audio guide free; ☻ 7.30am-5.30pm) contains a teahouse and small museum.

Find time for the **Suzhou Silk Museum** (苏州丝绸博物馆; 2001 Renmin Lu; 人民路2001号; admission Y15; ☻ 9am-5pm) and the **Suzhou Museum** (苏州博物馆; 204 Dongbei Jie; 东北街204号; admission free; ☻ 9am-5pm, last entry 4pm), which houses jade, ceramics, textiles and boasts a fabulous new building by IM Pei.

The lovely **West Garden Temple** (西园寺; Xiyuan Lu; 西园路; admission Y25; ☻ 8am-5.30am) is notable for its magnificent Arhat Hall, torched in 1860. The **Temple of Mystery** (玄妙观; Guanqian Jie; 观前街; admission Y10; ☻ 7.30am-5pm) lies at the centre of town. For views of town, climb the **North Temple Pagoda** (北寺塔; 1918 Renmin Lu; 人民路1918号; admission Y25; ☻ 7.45am-6pm).

Pan Gate (盘门; 1 Dong Dajie; 东大街1号; Pan Gate Y25; boat rides Y12; ☻ 7.30am-6pm) contains Suzhou's only remaining original city gate (dating from 1351).

INFORMATION

Location 85km west of Shanghai.

Getting there Express trains leave from Shanghai's main train station (Y15, 40 minutes, hourly 5.55am-7.51pm). Slow trains (one to two hours) run till midnight. Buses leave from both train stations (Y38, 1½ to two hours, half-hourly) and Pudong airport (Y84, three hours).

Getting around Get a bike at 371 Shiquan Jie (十全街; per day Y20, deposit Y300, ⌚ 8am-10pm).

Money Bank of China (中国银行; 1450 Renmin Lu; 人民路1450号; ⌚ 8.15am-5.15pm Mon-Fri) Also has a 24-hour ATM.

Sleeping Sheraton Suzhou (吴宫喜来登大酒店; ☎ 6510 3388; 259 Xinshi Lu; 新市路259号; s & d Y1880).

When to go All seasons; avoid public holidays.

Left Musician inside a hall of the Humble Administrator's Garden **Above** Garden of the Master of the Nets

EXCURSIONS

ZHUJIAJIAO

The delightful canal town of Zhujiajiao (pictured below) is easy to reach from Shanghai. Weekends are a crush, so aim for weekday visits. Being a historic town, what survives today is a charming tableau of Ming- and Qing-dynasty alleys, bridges and old-town architecture, so wander at will. Sights (admission Y30/60/80 for entry to 4/8/10 sights) include the **City God Temple** (城隍庙; admission Y5; ⏱ 7.30am-4pm) and the **Yuanjin Buddhist Temple** (圆津禅院; admission Y5; ⏱ 8am-4pm), near the distinctive **Tai'an Bridge** (泰安桥). Hunt out the peerless **Zhujiajiao Catholic Church of Ascension** (朱家角耶稣升天堂; 27 Caohe Jie, No 317 Alley; 漕河街27号317弄), dating from 1863, its belfry rising in a detached tower. Zhujiajiao's most photogenic bridge is **Fangsheng Bridge** (放生桥), first built in 1571. Jump on **boats** (per boat for 15/30mins Y60/120) for waterborne tours of the town at various points including Fangsheng Bridge.

INFORMATION
Location 30km west of Shanghai.
Getting there Buses (Y85, one hour) depart regularly from the Shanghai Sightseeing Bus Centre (p143) between 7.30am and noon. Tickets include admission to the town and most sights; last bus back to Shanghai is at 4.45pm. Buses (Y15.5, one hour) run to Zhujiajiao from Tongli.
When to go All seasons; avoid public holidays.

TONGLI

The canal town of Tongli (pictured below) is a marvellous day out from Shanghai. Much smaller than Suzhou, it's also more picturesque and easier to navigate. Zero in on the **Old Town** (古镇; admission Y80, excluding Chinese Sex Museum; ⏰ 7.30am-5.30pm), wander freely and don't worry about getting lost. The main sights are the **Gengle Tang** (耕乐堂), a huge Ming country residence with more than 40 rooms and courtyards. The **Pearl Pagoda** (珍珠塔) is another Ming-dynasty residence, but has no pagoda. The gorgeous **Tuisi Garden** (退思园) in the east of Tongli is perfect for drifting into pond-side reveries, tour groups permitting. Tongli's **Chinese Sex Museum** (中华性文化博物馆; admission Y20) is a well-publicised and fascinating foray into Chinese sexuality. For lazy waterborne sorties about the canals, hop on a six-person boat (Y70, 25 minutes). Restaurants are ubiquitous, as are guesthouses (客栈; *kezhan*).

INFORMATION

Location 80km west of Shanghai.
Getting there A bus departs from the Shanghai Sightseeing Bus Centre (p143; Y130, 1¾ hours) at 8.30am and leaves Tongli at 4.30pm.
When to go All seasons; avoid public holidays.

>SNAPSHOTS

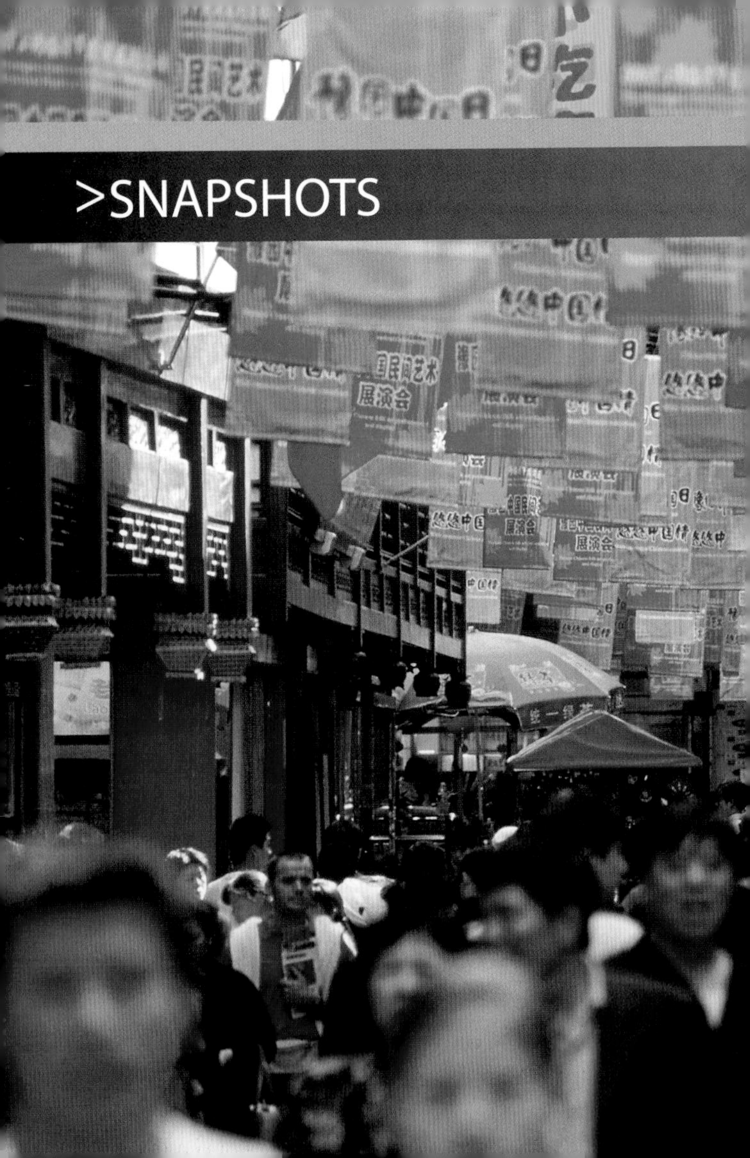

Shanghai is not just a city of individual sights; it's also a city of themes and subcultural interests where its various facets harmonise. Whatever the nature of your visit to Shanghai, let us help you access these different worlds and pursuits, and give you the lowdown on them all.

> Accommodation	118
> Architecture	120
> Food	122
> Drinking	124
> Fashion	126
> Silk & Antiques	127
> Massage & Spa Treatment	128
> Taichi & Chinese Martial Arts	129
> Art Galleries	130
> Markets	131
> Clubs	132
> Gay & Lesbian Shanghai	133
> Religion	134

Yuyuan Bazaar (p59)

SNAPSHOTS

ACCOMMODATION

Shanghai hotels range across all budgets. In a market that once saw marginal movement, nonstop construction and conversion over recent years has seen a huge number of new openings across all price categories, including smart new boutique hotels and dependable midrange chains. Except at the very best hotels and youth hostels, English-language skills are patchy.

Bar the landmark Peace Hotel (p42; undergoing much-needed renovation at the time of writing) and a handful of exclusive recent conversions, such as the **Mansion Hotel** (www.chinamansionhotel.com), most five-star hotels are global chains that offer a high standard of international service, but zero historic charm. Some of the more distinctive big hitters include the 15-storey art-deco **Peninsula** (www.peninsula.com), which was set to open on the Bund at the time this book went to press, and the **Park Hyatt Shanghai** (www.parkhyattshanghai.com), operating between the 79th to 93rd floors of the Shanghai World Financial Center, which is the world's highest hotel above ground level. Smaller boutique hotels, such as China's first carbon-neutral hotel, **Urbn** (www.urbnhotels.com), and B&B-style properties such as **Quintet** (www.quintet-shanghai.com), cluster around the French Concession and Jing'an.

Midrange hotels divide between converted historic buildings, run-of-the-mill Chinese hotels and, on the lower rung, formulaic but handy chain hotels. Rooms generally come with bath or shower, possibly broadband internet access and perhaps limited satellite TV. Midrange hotels are found in all neighbourhoods in Shanghai.

WEB RESOURCES

For hotel and flight bookings, **CTrip** (☎ 800 820 6666; http://english.ctrip.com) is an excellent online agency.

Need a place to stay? Find and book it at lonelyplanet.com. More than 80 properties are featured for Shanghai – each personally visited, thoroughly reviewed and happily recommended by a Lonely Planet author. From hostels to high-end hotels, we've hunted out the places that will bring you unique and special experiences. Read independent reviews by authors and other travellers, and get practical information including amenities, maps and photos. Then reserve your room simply and securely via Hotels & Hostels – our online booking service. It's all at lonelyplanet.com/hotels.

BEST HISTORIC HOTELS

> Astor House Hotel (浦江饭店;
  www.astorhousehotel.com)
> Mansion Hotel (首席公馆酒店;
  www.chinamansionhotel.com)
> Old House Inn (老时光酒店;
  www.oldhouse.cn)
> Peace Hotel (和平饭店;www
  .fairmont.com/peacehotel)

BEST STYLE ON A BUDGET

> Le Tour Traveler's Rest (乐途静
  安国际青年旅舍;www.letour
  shanghai.com)
> Ming Town E-Tour Youth Hostel (明
  堂青年旅社;www.yhachina.com)
> Ming Town Hiker Youth Hostel (明堂
  上海旅行者青年旅馆;www
  .yhachina.com)

BEST BOUTIQUE HOTELS

> Jia Shanghai (www.jiashanghai.com)
> Nine (Map pp64–5, B6; ☎ 6471
  9950; 355 West Jianguo Rd)
> Pudi Boutique Hotel (璞邸精品酒
  店; www.boutiquehotel.cc)
> Quintet (www.quintet-shanghai.com)
> Urbn (www.urbnhotels.com)

BEST ROOMS WITH A VIEW

> Grand Hyatt (金茂君悦大酒店;
  www.shanghai.grand.hyatt.com)
> JW Marriott Tomorrow Square
  (明天广场JW万怡酒店;www
  .marriott.com)
> Park Hyatt (柏悦酒店;www.park
  hyattshanghai.com)
> Peninsula (上海半岛酒店;www
  .peninsula.com)

Above The plush surrounds of Jia Shanghai

ARCHITECTURE

Like identical twins, Shanghai's sense of self as an erstwhile Paris of the East is inseparable from its architecture. The city is a stuffed treasure chest of architectural styles, from Buddhist temple architecture, Concession-era villas, homely alleyway houses, grandiose baroque banks and art deco apartment blocks to postmodern towers and dramatic skyscrapers topped with weird sci-fi protuberances. Whatever style floats your boat, Shanghai has it.

The British architectural firm Palmer & Turner designed many of Shanghai's landmark buildings in the 1920s, including the Hongkong & Shanghai Banking Corporation (HSBC) Building (p42), Customs House (p39) and Peace Hotel (p42). Buildings of this era were typically designed in neoclassical and baroque styles while the latter part of the decade saw the introduction of art deco (p15).

The Shanghai equivalent of Beijing's charming *hutong* alleyways and courtyard houses are its *lilong* (里弄; also called *longtang*, 弄堂) or alleys and the city's low-rise *shikumen* (石库门) or 'stone-gate houses'.

A distinctive blend of East and West, *shikumen* houses married the traditional Chinese courtyard house – with its interior courtyard features and emphasis on natural light – with the neat brickwork rows of English terrace housing. Between the 1850s and the 1940s, *shikumen* buildings made up 60% of Shanghai's housing.

Originally designed to house a single family, *shikumen* were usually only two to three storeys tall and fronted by an imposing stone gate frame topped with a decorated lintel that enclosed two stout, wooden doors. The lintel was sometimes elaborately carved with a dictum in Chinese, usually four characters long.

Since the 1980s a brave new world of architects has been refashioning the Shanghai skyline. Urban myth attests that over a quarter of the world's construction cranes were circling above Shanghai in the mid-1990s. The dramatic and modern Pudong skyline, along with parts of Puxi, is testament to the newfound optimism and confidence that now defines the city. The Jinmao Tower (p94), Shanghai World Financial Center (p94) and Tomorrow Square, as well as new edifices such as the White Magnolia Plaza (under construction), all reflect this resurgence which has completely transformed the architectural heritage of Shanghai in under two decades.

BEST MODERN BUILDINGS

> Jinmao Tower (p94)
> Oriental Art Center (p97)
> Oriental Pearl TV Tower (p94)
> Shanghai World Financial Center (p94)
> Shanghai South Train Station (p143)
> Suzhou Museum (p112)
> Tomorrow Square (near People's Square, p12)

BEST CONCESSION-ERA BUILDINGS

> Bank of China Building (p39)
> Hongkong & Shanghai Bank (p42)
> Peace Hotel (p42)
> Shanghai Art Museum (p43)

BEST SHIKUMEN ALLEYS

> Bubbling Well Lane, Jing'an (p90)
> Bubbling Well Road Apartments, Jing'an (p90)
> Shanyin Rd (near Lu Xun Memorial Hall), Hongkou (p106)
> Taikang Road Art Centre, French Concession (p66)

BEST TEMPLES OF WORSHIP

> Chenxiangge Nunnery (p56)
> Jade Buddha Temple (p83)
> Jing'an Temple (p83)
> St Ignatius Cathedral (p101)

Above The futuristic Tomorrow Square, located near People's Square (p12)

FOOD

Shanghai is the white-hot crucible of China's economic makeover, and the fizzing sense of excitement also fires up its kitchens. Chefs from all over China and abroad have crowded in to add their flavours to the mix. If you want Chinese, there's no better place to be. The Chinatown schlock you get at home is at best a pale imitation of Cantonese food, which is a bit like eating steak and kidney pie and thinking that's the best Europe can offer. China's a big, big place. Luckily, its flavours converge in Shanghai. You don't have to trek to far-flung Kashgar for Uighur *laghman* (pulled noodles) or Lanzhou for the Gansu take on the same. Manchurian restaurants have come to town so there's no need to hoof it to Harbin, while Yunnan chefs have shuttled in from Kunming. Dishes have even made it to Shanghai from the roof of the world. Peking duck long ago waddled into town and you only have to snack around to sample some of China's best-loved snacks and nibbles. And you can't come to Shanghai without trying its own, celebrated local cuisine. Restaurants range from the exclusive ones, where starched table linen, top-notch food and meticulous waiting staff create an extravagant performance, to the smallest hole-in-the-wall (小吃; *xiaochi*) down a side street, where requests for a menu (English or Chinese) are met with blank looks. In between, a colourful panoply of eateries that cater to all budgets and culinary instincts can be found. Don't be afraid to experiment – this is what travel is all about. Pop into a restaurant and if you can't read the menu, use our menu decoder (p147), flap your chopsticks at the dish you want, or take it as an operational Chinese lesson.

BEST SHANGHAINESE
> Bai's Restaurant (p78)
> Baoluo Jiuluo (p78)
> Fu 1039 (p87)
> Jishi Jiulou (p78)
> Lynn (p88)
> Yang's Fry Dumplings (p48)

BEST REGIONAL CHINESE
> Crystal Jade (p68)
> Di Shui Dong (p69)
> Dongbei Ren (p69)
> Lost Heaven (p79)
> Sichuan Citizen (p79)
> Xindalu (p108)

BEST FUSION FOOD
> Factory (p108)
> Jean Georges (p46)
> T8 (p70)

BEST VEGETARIAN
> Gongdelin (p46)
> Longhua Temple (p100)
> Jade Buddha Temple (p83)
> Qimin Organic Hotpot (p88)
> Songyuelou (p60)
> Vegetarian Lifestyle (p70, p88)

Left Nanxiang Steamed Bun Restaurant (p60) **Above** Street food in Hongkou (p104)

DRINKING

In a nod to its debauched and drug-addled past, alcohol runs through Shanghai's veins in generous quantities. Perhaps more than any other city in China, without its bars, this city would have a social and emotional wasteland. Well-financed, hard-working and homesick expats see Shanghai's drinking culture as an indispensable ally, and watering holes occupy the very hub of expat social life.

But while bars and pubs are frequented predominantly by foreigners, the race is on to capture the domestic market. In Beijing there's a more populist approach – Y15 Tsingtaos and unpretentious watering holes – but Shanghai has stayed true to its roots: it's all about looking flash, sipping glam cocktails and tapping into the insatiable appetite for new trends. As might be expected, new bars pop up and disappear again with impressive rapidity – any bar older than a decade is an old-timer. But the upside to the intense competition is that weekly specials and happy hours (generally from 5pm to 8pm) manage to keep Shanghai affordable, at least in relation to cities outside of China.

Cafe culture is the latest trend to sweep Shanghai – cafes are more popular than bars – and while you'd be hard pressed to find a decent teahouse within a 20km radius, cappuccinos and sandwiches served at hip wireless hangouts – some familiar names, some not – are all over the place. Another common sight are the street stalls selling *zhenzhu naicha* (bubble tea), a strangely addictive Taiwanese milk tea with tapioca balls, and all sorts of related spin-offs, such as hot ginger drinks or freshly puréed mango smoothies.

Bars usually open late afternoon (but many open earlier) and call it a night at around 2am.

BEST BARS WITH A VIEW
> Captain's Bar (p49)
> Cloud 9 (p97)
> Fat Olive (p60)
> New Heights (p50)

BEST BARS FOR POSING
> Bar Rouge (p48)
> DR Bar (p70)
> Glamour Bar (p50)
> TMSK (p70)

BEST CAFES
> Bund 12 Café (p49)
> Cafe 85°C (p88)
> Citizen Café (p70)
> Wagas (p90)

Left Dazzling views from Bar Rouge (p48) **Above** Stylish TMSK bar (p70)

FASHION

Shanghai has its own crop of local designers stitching the city into the world fashion map. There are boutiques everywhere in the French Concession, but around the South Shanxi Rd metro station are a few blocks of micro-sized new-concept shops that are particularly worth seeking out. Young designers have taken over a one-block stretch of Changle Rd (Map pp64–5, D1) east of Ruijin No 1 Rd: check out La Vie (p75) for Jenny Ji's stylish take on street fashion, Elbis Hungi (p75) for jeans, eno (p75) for custom T-shirts and One by One (p75) for a trio of local designers. The two-block stretch of Xinle Rd (Map pp64–5, B2) has less high-end fashion than Changle Rd, but ultimately greater variety. Pop into the Thing (p75) for Chinglish T-shirts, 100 Change & Insect (p67) for shoes and Source (p75) for a taste of the 'Hai's urban style. Bargain hunters should look for Junmeizu (p75) around the corner. Other local brands, such as Insh (p67), Urban Tribe and Shirt Flag (p67), can be found at the Taikang Road Art Centre. Xintiandi (p68) is also a good stop, with upmarket creations from Shanghai Trio, NoD and Annabel Lee. Most small stores open their doors around noon and stay open until 10pm.

Feel Shanghai (p68), Taikang Road Art Centre

SILK & ANTIQUES

Silk and tailored clothing are good value in Shanghai. For tailor-making and a wide range of silk, **Silk King** (真丝大王; www.silkking.com) has several branches, selling silk from Y158 per metre, as well as silk clothing and providing quick custom tailoring. The Shiliupu Fabric Market (p59) is several floors of inexpensive silks, fabrics and custom tailoring. For figure-hugging *qipao* (cheongsam), pop over to the boutiques along Changle Rd (between South Maoming Rd and South Shaanxi Rd), South Maoming Rd and the Taikang Road Art Centre (p68).

It's only natural that visitors to Shanghai keep an eye out for bargain antiques. There's always the powerful hope that you'll unearth the late Yuan dynasty *qinghua* vase that will take care of the mortgage. Most antiques of any worth have already long been identified, however, and are priced accordingly. If you do chance upon a cheap Guangxu-reign imperial yellow, you can bet your bottom *yuan* it's a forgery (仿古; *fanggu*).

If, however, you are willing to pay for a genuine piece, Shanghai is not short of antique shops. There are several good-quality antique shops and warehouses out west near the Hongqiao airport, principally selling late Ming- and Qing-dynasty furniture. Always ask if a piece has been restored, as it's common to find cabinets or chests that have been professionally patched up. If a piece was made prior to 1795, it cannot be exported. For art-deco antiques, shop at Art Deco (p86).

Dongtai Road Antique Market (p58)

MASSAGE & SPA TREATMENT

In the 17th and 18th centuries, Qing-dynasty barbers developed the current form of Chinese massage, known as *tuina* (推拿; literally 'push-grab'). In addition to cutting hair, skilled barbers learned to use acupressure points to treat different ailments and the practice, which was cheaper, less painful and safer than acupuncture, soon became quite popular. The general idea behind Chinese massage is that it stimulates your *qì* (vital energy that flows along different pathways or meridians, each of which is connected to a major organ) and removes energy blockages, though of course it is often used to treat specific ailments, from muscular and joint pain to the common cold.

In Shanghai, getting a quality body or foot massage has never been easier, and they come at a fraction of the price that you'd pay at home. **Dragonfly** (www.dragonfly.net.cn) and **Green Massage** (www.greenmassage.com.cn) are two of the massage parlours with numerous branches around town.

Also look out for blind massage parlours, where body and foot massages are conducted by skilled blind masseurs. Try **Lulu Massage** (璐潞盲人按摩中心; Map pp64–5, C4; ☎ 6473 2634; 597 Middle Fuxing Rd; 复兴中路597号; ❤ noon-1am).

For full-on pampering, Shanghai's spas (many top international hotels have one) can also take you to another level of serenity.

Indulge yourself at Dragonfly

TAICHI & CHINESE MARTIAL ARTS

Dreaming of upending hardened Karate 4th *dan* black belts with a mere shrug? Itching to master the devastating eight palm changes of Bagua Zhang? Now is your chance. Learning martial arts for many young Chinese is about as sexy as watching paint dry, but for Westerners, the mind-bending antics of Bruce Lee and Jackie Chan have fired up generations of eager hopefuls. Shanghai may not be Wudang Shan, but fighting talent exists.

Taichi is often labelled as an exercise system, but it is also a Taoist martial art, with punches, kicks, locks and weapons. The road to skill is long and arduous, but scaling the learning curve is rewarding. Taichi teaches the body to fully relax and maximise its inherent strength, improves balance and flexibility and exercises the joints, while strengthening the legs. The short Yang style may look easy to perform, but the Chen style is simply agonising.

Other Taoist arts to look out for are Xingyi Quan ('form-mind boxing'), Bagua Zhang ('eight-trigram palm') and the more vigorous Buddhist Shaolin styles. Good places to look for teachers and students are Shanghai's parks, first thing in the morning. See also the websites of these martial arts schools: **Longwu Kungfu Center** (www.longwukungfu.com), **Oz Body Fit** (www.ozbodyfit.com) and **Mingwu International Kungfu** (www.mingwukungfu.com).

Practising taichi on the Bund promenade (p38)

V

SNAPSHOTS

ART GALLERIES

Like everything else in Shanghai, Chinese art is a commodity being increasingly vacuumed up by wealthy investors and foreign art hunters. Before you assume there's a genuine artistic revolution out there, it's worth noting the tendency for gallery-hung Chinese art to absorb Western needs and expectations like a multicoloured sponge. With all the money sloshing around, gallery owners find themselves promoting artists with the slimmest evidence of talent. Originality is frequently starved and there's still too much pop and not enough hop: the constant ironic artistic references to wealth, communism, propaganda and consumerism in Shanghai art can grate. But it also means that Shanghai is hardly short of galleries.

If buying, you will need to know your market and prepare to see unaccomplished work. Exploring Shanghai's galleries will bring you face-to-face with an art form that experiences less censorship than other media, including cinema. This paradoxically makes Chinese art both exhilarating and dull; PRC art pushes the envelope, but in a predictable and limited direction.

Like Beijing's wildly successful 798 Art District, the M50 Art Centre (p21) is a converted former factory area. Its bright and spacious proletarian workshops are transformed into trendy art galleries, shops and cafes.

BEST ART GALLERIES
> Art Labor (p66)
> Art Scene (at M50, p83)
> Factory (p108)
> island6 (at M50, p83)
> James Cohan (p66)
> Propaganda Poster Art Centre (p74)
> Shanghai Gallery of Art (p43)
> ShanghART (p63)

BEST ART MUSEUMS
> Shanghai Museum (p43)
> Shanghai Museum of Contemporary Art (p43)
> Zendai Museum of Modern Art (p96)

MARKETS

For variety and the best deals, roll up your sleeves at Shanghai's markets (市场; *shichang*). At clothing, souvenir and antiques markets, haggling (see p150) is the norm. The number of vendors also means you can easily browse and compare prices. It is unlikely vendors will exchange goods, but check when you buy. You will generally be able to use only cash, but keep your money in inside pockets when visiting places such as Qipu Market (p107), where pickpockets can pose as pushy vendors. Don't overlook ferreting along Shanghai's **Flower, Bird & Insect Market** (万商花鸟鱼虫市场; pictured below) on South Xizang Rd, just north of the intersection with West Fangbang Rd, to the west of the Old Town. In all their slithering glory, Shanghai's wet markets (for fish, animals and vegetables) are mesmerising, but can be gory. One worthwhile wet market to check out is the Tanggu Rd (塘沽路) market in Hongkou.

BEST SOUVENIR MARKETS

> Dongtai Road Antique Market (p58)
> Fuyou Antique Market (p58)
> Old Street (p58)
> Yuyuan Bazaar (p59)

BEST CLOTHING MARKETS

> AP Xinyang Fashion & Gifts Market (p96)
> Fenshine Fashion & Accessories Plaza (p86)
> Qipu Market (p107)
> Shiliupu Fabric Market (p59)
> Wangjia Docks Fabric Market (p59)

CLUBS

Although the clubbing scene remains in its adolescence, the sheer demand for a good time and cutting-edge experimentation brings out Shanghai's variety and inventiveness (and occasional garishness). The city's swift transition from dead zone to party central forges an inventive clubbing attitude and a constant stream of clubbers. As with bars, however, Shanghai's effervescent clubs often have a short shelf life, arriving and departing with metronome-like regularity. Sounds and clubs are international and Chinese; the latter is more popular with the local crowd. Clubs range from huge, swanky spaces dedicated to the preening Hong Kong and white-collar crowd to more relaxed and intimate spots plus trendy bars that rustle up weekend DJs. Club weekend ticket prices offer good value, typically in the Y100 region, with a drink. For a full and au-courant list of clubs, pick up a copy of *That's Shanghai* or click on www.smartshanghai.com. Karaoke is a local subculture that packs in crowds fighting to grab the golden microphone. If you're in Shanghai on business, expect to be forced into a karaoke parlour and joyfully presented with the song menu (there's usually a decent crop of English songs) as you clear your throat and reach for the strong stuff. For gay and lesbian bars and clubs, see opposite.

Start with cocktails, then hit the dance floor at Zapata's (p80)

GAY & LESBIAN SHANGHAI

The Shanghai gay scene is disconcertingly low-profile: the Chinese are a naturally undemonstrative people, their culture is conservative and the Communists put gay pride way down their wish list. With considerable stigma attached to homosexuality (both at home and in the workplace), openly coming out is far more difficult in Chinese society than it is elsewhere in the world. Stir in the government's promotion of ethical socialism and communist prudence, and gay parades along East Nanjing Rd are an unlikely fixture. Yet, as a pulsating, cosmopolitan and rapidly liberalising city, Shanghai is a natural destination for China's gays and lesbians. Venues to look out for include D2 at Cool Docks (p58), currently the big dance club; **Frangipani** (Map pp84-5, F5; ☎ 5375 0084; 399 Dagu Rd; 大沽路399号; ⏰ 6pm-2am), a laid-back lounge for girls and guys; and **Shanghai Studio** (Map p73, B5; ☎ 6283 1043; www.shanghai-studio.com; No 4, Lane 1950, Middle Huaihai Rd; 淮海中路1950弄4号; ⏰ 9pm-2am) and **Eddy's Bar** (Map p73, B5; ☎ 6282 0521; 1877 Middle Huaihai Rd; 淮海中路1877号; ⏰ 8pm-2am Mon-Thu, to 3am Fri-Sun).

Do not mistake same-sex hand-holding as a sign of sexual orientation – young Chinese men often drape their arms around each other's shoulders or stand physically close to each other. *City Weekend* runs a bimonthly gay and lesbian column.

RELIGION

To be spellbound by Shanghai's consumer madness is to ignore much of what modern China is about. To get a feel for the Chinese as people, it is vital to have an understanding of their devotional impulses. Religious observation has enjoyed a startling renaissance in Shanghai and the rest of China since the end of Mao Zedong's leadership. Of course, while religious freedom exists in China, this is freedom with Chinese characteristics. Belief systems, such as Falun Gong, can be banned overnight.

China has a long history of importing faiths and beliefs (Buddhism, Christianity, Judaism, Islam, Communism), but it is surely Christianity that is making the most converts among modern Chinese. Proselytising may be banned, but this hasn't slowed the spread of the Christian gospel (*hao xiaoxi*) as legions including Shanghainese turn to Christianity. The Middle Eastern faith has had a toe-hold in China since the 8th century (with the arrival of the Nestorians) but its standing has always been precarious, until recent years. Christianity may be in decline in the West, but it has found new impetus in China, partly because associations are made by the Chinese between the religion and developed-world status of many Christian nations.

The best way to encounter religious observance is to visit the city's temples. Some shrines, such as the former Tianhou Temple, have been obliterated, but a considerable crop survives to the present.

BEST BUDDHIST TEMPLES

> Chenxiangge Nunnery (p56)
> Jade Buddha Temple (p83)
> Lingyin Temple (p110)
> Yuanjin Buddhist Temple (p114)

BEST TAOIST TEMPLES

> Temple of Mystery (p112)
> Temple of the Town God (p56)

BEST CHURCHES

> Catholic Church, Qibao (p100)
> St Ignatius Cathedral (p101)
> St Nicholas Church (p66)
> Zhujiajiao Catholic Church of Ascension (p114)

>BACKGROUND

BACKGROUND

HISTORY

The boggy marshland of Shanghai did not emerge as a town of note until the late 13th century, when it became a county seat as part of Jiangsu. A wall was erected around the town in the mid-16th century to deter Japanese pirates and, by the end of the next century, a population of 50,000 was living off cotton production, fishing and trade in tea and silk.

The seeds of Shanghai as an international trading hub were not sown until the Qing dynasty (1644–1912), when British traders based in Canton (Guangzhou) began importing opium into China to trade for silver, thus correcting a marked trade imbalance. The highly addictive drug rapidly permeated all levels of Chinese society with *hongs* (trading houses) such as Jardine Matheson, built upon its trade.

Smouldering friction between Great Britain and China over the drug finally erupted in the conflict fought in its name: the First Opium War. The Treaty of Nanking (1842) that concluded the hostilities opened five ports, including Shanghai and Canton, to the West.

Great Britain's arrival in Shanghai, dating from 1843, was soon followed by other nations, including France and the United States. Trade quickly flourished as the area outside the Old Town was divided into British, French and American Concessions. Trade of silk, tea, textiles, porcelain and opium was matched by rapidly developing banking, insurance and real-estate sectors. China and the West traded with each other via Chinese middlemen called compradors (from the Portuguese). Lured by the sense of opportunity, a growing swell of immigrants from other parts of China began to arrive. The city found itself propelled into a modern era of gaslight, electricity and cars.

Meanwhile, the West's impact on China was having other effects. The Christian-inspired Taiping Rebellion swept to east China from Guangxi, establishing its capital in Nanjing in 1854. Suzhou and Hangzhou both fell to Taiping rebels, but Shanghai survived, despite the activities of the Taiping-affiliated Small Swords Society in the Old Town.

The Taiping Rebellion inundated Shanghai with refugees seeking sanctuary in the foreign Concessions. The resulting housing and construction boom led to the development of Shanghai's characteristic *lilong* (alleyways) and *shikumen* (stone-gate houses) (p20).

The 19th century closed with the xenophobic Boxer Uprising – inspired by a sense of national humiliation at the hands of the foreign powers – and hence the rapid weakening of Manchu (Qing) authority. The revolt of 1911 lead to the downfall of the Qing dynasty and the formation of the short-lived Republic. Shanghai joined the revolt but stuck to its creed of making money while the rest of China gradually slipped into the ensuing chaos of feuding warlords.

Shanghai's social ills, such as its yawning economic disparities, its unbridgeable Chinese and foreign divisions, and escalating crime, debauchery and vice, fostered the circulation of radical political sentiments. Foreign ideas flowed into Shanghai, finding fertile ground in the city's growing ranks of writers and political thinkers. The *Communist Manifesto* was translated into Chinese, finding an avid audience among those agitating for change. Attended by Mao Zedong, the first meeting of the Chinese Communist Party was held in July 1921 in a French Concession house (see p63). Meanwhile, anti-Western sentiment intensified after British soldiers killed 12 Chinese during a demonstration.

Chiang Kaishek wrested control of Shanghai from a warlord in March 1927, an event soon followed by his 'White Terror', when thousands of Communists, left-wing sympathisers and labour leaders were slaughtered, with the collusion of gangster Du Yuesheng ('big eared' Du) and his men.

The Shanghai of the 1930s was a world of great vigour, the latest fashions, incredible architecture, crime and vice, which turned the city into the 'Paris of the East' and its seedy flip side, the 'Whore of the Orient'. By 1934 Shanghai was the world's fifth-largest city, its population of three million swelled by an influx of immigrants, including Russians and Jews.

Japan's invasion of China in 1937 followed its occupation of Manchuria in 1931 and the destruction of Shanghai's Zhapei (Zhabei) district. Shanghai fell to the Japanese in 1937, who proceeded to prosecute their notorious Rape of Nanjing that December. After the Japanese surrender in 1945, the civil war between the Kuomintang under Chiang Kaishek and the Communists under Mao Zedong led to a Nationalist retreat to Taiwan in 1949 and the establishment of the People's Republic of China on 1 October 1949. By this time, foreigners had already deserted Shanghai and its Concession days were over.

The Communists closed Shanghai's brothels, re-educated its prostitutes and eradicated the slums. Shanghai, eager to prove its communist credentials, established a short-lived commune during the anarchic Cultural Revolution (1966–1976).

The death of Mao Zedong in 1976 paved the way for the rehabilitation of Deng Xiaoping, architect of the liberating reform policy and opening up that was to position Shanghai back in the international limelight. Shanghai's most defining modern moment arrived in 1990 when Pudong became a Special Economic Zone. By the mid-1990s up to half of the world's high-rise cranes were present as the dazzling Shanghai of today – with its two airports, rapidly expanding metro system, massive bridges, vast web of flyovers and skyscrapers – took shape.

LIFE AS A SHANGHAI RESIDENT

Shanghai has a strong regional identity, forged from its unique history, dialect and geographic location. In many respects, however, the Shanghainese are similar to the Hong Kong Chinese: both are southern Chinese from flourishing coastal towns that historically served as havens for refugees and embraced Western customs and beliefs. Like the Hong Kong Chinese, the Shanghainese are physically shorter and thinner than their taller and stockier northern brethren.

The Shanghainese are admired by other Chinese for their competence and envied for their material successes. On the downside, they are also seen by their compatriots as being stingy, petty, calculating, unfriendly and demanding.

Shanghai has long flirted with the Western perspective, but the city remains staunchly Chinese in its traditions and customs. Like all Chinese, the Shanghainese are proud of their Chinese ancestry; concessions to Western taste are often no more than a theatrical device. The *average* Shanghai resident actually has little exposure to the West beyond the TV set, and will speak no English. It's easy to overlook, but virtually no tourists left China prior to 1979 and only in very recent years have visitor numbers to the West slowly grown. China – including Shanghai – remains introspective.

Shanghai dreams of being a cosmopolitan city, but a simple comparison between Pudong International Airport and, say, Kuala Lumpur International Airport catches, in miniature, the startling difference between the two cities. Shanghai's international airport has none of the multicultural buzz and effortless internationalism and multilingualism of Kuala Lumpur's flight hub. Cosmopolitanism in Shanghai can appear forced and unnatural, and this is partly the legacy of earlier Communist days. Despite surface impressions, Shanghai is becoming more Chinese rather than increasingly international, as vast numbers of domestic immigrants pour into town.

SHANGHAI DOS & SHANGHAI DON'TS

> Always offer to take your shoes off when entering a Chinese person's home.
> When presenting your business card, proffer it with the first finger and thumb of both hands (thumbs on top).
> Don't ram your chopsticks vertically into your rice, but lay them down on your plate or on the chopstick rest.
> Always hand your cigarettes around in social situations.
> Don't insist on paying the dinner or bar bill if your fellow diner appears determined.
> Biting your fingernails is a no-no.
> Losing face *(diumianzi)* is about making the Chinese look stupid or being forced to back down in front of others. Take care to avoid it and don't lose sight of your own face in the process.

Employment, health care, education and property prices are major concerns for both young families and retired workers. House prices have rocketed since the 1990s (although the market sagged in 2005 after an antispeculation sales tax was imposed) and although property prices on average are not as high as those in Europe or the US, salaries in Shanghai are far, far lower. With vast salary disparities and no ways to effect political change, the Shanghainese can do little but harness their ambitions. Well-paid white-collar employees in their 30s can make Y30,000 a month (plus perks), while at simple takeaway restaurants chefs can expect to earn only around Y1000 to Y2500 per month, and a cashier Y800 to Y1200. Except for those in the top salary bracket, buying a flat is merely a dream.

ART & ARCHITECTURE

ART

Shanghai has blossomed artistically since the grey 1980s, but creativity in this cosmopolitan metropolis remains in a curious state of dwarfism and neglect. As elsewhere in China, the education system fails to nurture originality or a questioning creativity in children and restraints are put on thinking outside the box. When examining the arts scene in Shanghai, remember that the Chinese are also deeply conformist. Pressures on Shanghai's citizens to make money and eschew the artistic path result in a lack of artistic boldness. Nonetheless, art is often more political in content than other creative fields (such as literature), shielded by its oblique content and ambiguities. The increasing numbers of art galleries (p130) suggests a commercial renaissance and a growing appetite for art.

ARCHITECTURE

Shanghai has China's most diverse array of architectural styles (p120), exceeding even Hong Kong or Macau. Wandering Shanghai's streets is the best way to get a taste of its eclectic architectural brew, which ranges from traditional temple architecture through art deco, neoclassical, socialist, postmodern, postsocialist and then into uncharted territory.

By far the most elegant and charming district is the French Concession, with its art-deco apartment blocks, villas and cottages. Shanghai's urban textures are far from uniform and brushed aluminium shop fronts regularly give way to bruised streetscapes of fractured paving slabs and grimy apartment blocks that suggest both the inequalities of wealth and a city fast outstripping itself. The city's swish districts are in the pink, but the suburbs are grey, featureless sprawls of housing blocks and concrete streets.

The city has grown too fast and too furiously, and the skyline is an incongruous mix that is at once impressive and disorienting. It's futuristic yet dated, exciting yet frightening, and it's continuing to change at MagLev speed.

GOVERNMENT & POLITICS

The People's Republic of China is governed by the Chinese Communist Party (CCP), with President Hu Jintao at its head.

As one of China's four municipalities, Shanghai is headed by a mayor. The city long served as a torch-bearer for radical ideas and protesting sentiments, acting as a weathervane for the national mood. These days, however, the city is increasingly cocooned within its own spectacular growth figures and many Chinese say that it is out of touch with the rest of China, especially the rural peasantry.

Wary of its economic power, Beijing is increasingly keen to clip Shanghai's wings. The city's former party secretary Chen Liangyu was sacked for corruption in 2006, sentenced to 18 years in prison and replaced by a Hu Jintao ally.

ECONOMY

With its spectacular geographic location and unique history as one of China's first cities to open to Western trade, Shanghai has long been aware of its economic advantages.

With a staggering GDP of US$200 billion, the Shanghai region – combined with the neighbouring provinces of Jiangsu and Zhejiang – accounts for almost a third of China's total exports. Its economy continued to expand during the recession, highlighting Shanghai's position as one of the world's economic powerhouses.

The Shanghainese excel at making money. Beijing folk may be generous, erudite and invariably hospitable, but it's the Shanghainese who focus their energies exclusively on wealth creation. The latest hot stocks and tips are text-messaged about town at high velocity as moneymakers play the stock market.

Shanghai is not, however, some kind of city state like Singapore. It is not even a Hong Kong operating under the 'One Country, Two Systems' arrangement. It is an intrinsic part of China and, as such, it is buffeted by the social and political currents that course the land.

Pessimists argue that China's current growth model is shaky. Will Hutton's incisive *The Writing on the Wall* is the latest well-argued forecast of China's unsustainable growth curve. Try to get a copy of Kerry Brown's excellent *Struggling Giant: China in the 21st Century*, in which the author applies his rich experience living and working in China to determine (in often humorous fashion) the startling incongruities of this land. *Mr China: A Memoir* by Tim Clissold is a hysterically honest account of how to lose money big time in China.

ENVIRONMENT

To deflate suspicions that China is a major environmental polluter, Shanghai is hosting Expo 2010 with a focus on sustainable development. Visitors might find it inconceivable that Shanghai has any sort of environmental credentials going for it (cough, cough) but, looking back at the past 20 years, the city actually has made some progress on this front. Suzhou Creek just finished a decade-long clean-up and air pollution is slightly better (at least at the levels of airborne toxins), with major factories moved out of town. But significant challenges await both the city and country, particularly with regards to energy use.

FURTHER READING
NONFICTION
In Search of Old Shanghai By Lynn Pan (aka Pan Ling). A historical rummage through Shanghai's heydays.
Life and Death in Shanghai By Nien Cheng. This is a classic account of the Cultural Revolution, using Shanghai as its setting.

Shanghai By Harriet Sergeant. A lively historic portrait of the city and its people when it was at the height of its powers in the 1920s and 1930s.

Shanghai: The Rise and Fall of a Decadent City 1842–1949 By Stella Dong. A well-written, captivating sketch of the city that entrances the reader with its colour and anecdotes.

The Bund Shanghai: China Faces West By Peter Hibbard. For architecture buffs, this book gives a full checklist of the history and phantoms of the Bund's buildings.

FICTION

Candy By Mian Mian. A trendy novel that depicts life, sex and drugs in Shenzhen and Shanghai.

Death of a Red Heroine By Qiu Xiaolong. Despite stilted dialogue, this well-received crime novel offers a street-level view of the changes engulfing Shanghai in the 1990s.

Empire of the Sun By JG Ballard. A highly acclaimed tale based on the author's internment as a child in a Japanese prisoner-of-war camp in Shanghai.

Lust, Caution By Eileen Chang. Chang earned the everlasting disapproval of her politically minded peers with this tragic novella, in which love betrays the Revolution.

When We Were Orphans By Kazuo Ishiguro. An English detective heads to Shanghai to discover the truth behind his parents' disappearance.

FILMS

Code 46 By Michael Winterbottom. A love story set in a dystopian future, with Shanghai as the urban backdrop.

Empire of the Sun By Stephen Spielberg. Celebrated adaptation of JG Ballard's poignant tale (above).

Lust, Caution By Ang Lee. This sensuous remake of Eileen Chang's spy thriller (above), set during the Japanese occupation, is arguably better than the book.

Shanghai Triad By Zhang Yimou. A Fifth Generation masterpiece, starring Gong Li, that delves into Shanghai's 1930s gangster underworld.

Suzhou River By Ye Lou. A brooding reflection on love in gritty, modern Shanghai.

Temptress Moon By Chen Kaige. Opium addiction, more gangsters and emotional manipulation – another Gong Li classic, set in the 1930s.

The Painted Veil By John Curran. Excellent period tale of a marital crisis unfolding against the backdrop of 1920s Shanghai and cholera-infested Guangxi province, starring Edward Norton and Naomi Watts.

DIRECTORY
TRANSPORT
ARRIVAL & DEPARTURE
AIR
Pudong International Airport 浦东国际机场

Pudong International Airport (☎ 6834 1000, flight information 96990; www .shairport.com; 📶) is located 30km southeast of Shanghai, near the East China Sea. Most visitors arrive in Shanghai at this airport. Departures are on the upper level and arrivals are on the lower level, where there's a tourist information counter. Pick up a free map before the baggage hall; ATMs are on both sides of customs.

Hongqiao Airport 虹桥机场

Hongqiao airport (☎ 6268 8899, flight information in English & Chinese 5260 4620; www.shairport.com; 📶) serves domestic destinations.

BUS
Tour buses to Suzhou, Hangzhou, Tongli, Zhujiajiao and other destinations around Shanghai depart from the Shanghai Sightseeing Bus Centre (上海旅游集散中心; Map p99, C4) at Shanghai Stadium.

TRAIN
Trains depart to destinations all over China from **Shanghai train station** (上海火车站; Map pp84-5, F1; 385 Meiyuan Rd) and **Shanghai South train station** (上海南站; 200 Zhaofeng Rd), although fewer numbers of visitors arrive this way. When buying tickets, check which station your train departs from.

VISA
Apart from citizens from Japan, Singapore and Brunei, a visa is required for all visitors to China. Visas can be obtained from Chinese embassies and consulates. Most

---

CLIMATE CHANGE & TRAVEL
Travel – especially air travel – is a significant contributor to global climate change. At Lonely Planet, we believe that all who travel have a responsibility to limit their personal impact. As a result, we have teamed with Rough Guides and other concerned industry partners to support Climate Care, which allows people to offset the greenhouse gases they are responsible for with contributions to energy-saving projects and other climate-friendly initiatives in the developing world. Lonely Planet offsets all staff and author travel.

For more information, turn to the responsible travel pages on www.lonelyplanet .com. For details on offsetting your carbon emissions and a carbon calculator, go to www .climatecare.org.

tourists get a single-entry visa for a 30-day stay, valid for three months from the date of issue.

Your passport must be valid for at least six months after the expiry date of your visa; at least one entire blank page in your passport is required for the visa.

GETTING AROUND
TRAVEL PASSES
A handy transport card (交通 卡) is sold at metro stations and some convenience stores; cards can be topped up and used on the metro, taxis and most buses. Deposits for the card are Y25; refunds are available at the East

Nanjing Rd metro station (Map pp40–1). Buying the card does not save you money, but saves queuing for tickets on the metro. Tourist passes (Y25), offering unlimited one-day travel on the metro, may be introduced by the time this book is in print.

BUS
Despite having 1000 routes, the bus system is torturous for non-Chinese-speaking passengers. Bus stop signs and routes are in Chinese only, and drivers and conductors speak little if any English, although on-board announcements in English help. Buses cost

Transport Options To/From Pudong International Airport

	Taxi	Metro Line 2
Pick-up point	Central Shanghai	Hongqiao airport
Drop-off point	Door-to-door service	Pudong International Airport
Duration	60min	
Other	Use official taxi queue	Stops in Pudong, People's Sq, Jing'an
Cost	Y140; use meter	Y3-7

Transport Options To/From Hongqiao Airport

	Taxi	Metro Line 2
Pick-up point	Bund	Hongqiao Airport
Drop-off point	Door-to-door service	Pudong International Airport
Duration	30-60min	
Other	Long taxi queues at airport	Stops in Pudong, People's Sq, Jing'an
Cost	Y60	Y3-7

Y2 to Y3 and generally operate from 5am to 11pm.

CAR
As you require a residency permit to drive in Shanghai, short-stay tourists are effectively barred from hiring cars in Shanghai.

FERRY
Several ferries cross the Huangpu River between Puxi and Pudong, and 12 new docks were expected to be added for the World Expo (remaining in operation afterward), though the new routes were not yet public at press time. The most useful ferry operates

between the southern end of the Bund and Pudong (Y2).

METRO
The city's metro trains are easily the best way to get around Shanghai. They are fast, cheap and clean, although don't count on getting a seat. There should be 11 lines in operation by the time this book is in print – up from three lines in 2003!

The most useful lines for travellers are 1, 2 and 10. Line 1 connects the two train stations, passing through People's Square and the French Concession. Line 2 connects the two airports and passes through Pudong, East

Bus 2	Bus 5	MagLev
Jing'an Temple	Shanghai train station	Metro line 2, Longyang Rd
Outside Arrivals/Departures halls	Outside Arrivals/Departures halls	Pudong International Airport
60min	70min	8min
	Bus stop is near People's Sq	Taxi from terminus to city about Y40
Y22	Y16-22	Y40 with same-day air ticket

Airport Shuttle Bus	Bus 925	Airport Bus Line 1
Arrivals Hall	Arrivals Hall	Arrivals Hall
Jing'an Temple	People's Sq	Pudong International Airport
35min	60min	minimum 60min
Leaving every 15min		Leaving every 20-30min
Y4	Y4	Y30

Nanjing Rd (the Bund) and Jing'an. Lines 1 and 2 connect at the People's Square interchange, the busiest of all stations. Line 10 will run through the French Concession, the Old Town, the Bund area and Hongkou.

Tickets range from Y3 to Y7 depending on the distance; they are only sold from the automated machines. Keep your ticket until you exit. Most trains run from about 6am to 10.30pm. Stops are announced in English as well as Chinese. To find a metro station look for the red 'M'.

TAXI

Shanghai's 45,000 air-conditioned taxis are reasonably cheap and hassle-free, and they're easy to flag down outside rush hour, although finding a cab during rain storms is impossible. Many taxis have no rear seatbelts, so sit up front. Flag fall is Y11 for the first 3km, and Y2 per kilometre thereafter; there is no need to tip. A night rate operates from 11pm to 5am, when the flag fall is Y14, then Y2.6 per kilometre. If you don't speak Chinese, have your destination written down in characters. Also take your mobile phone (see p88). Shanghai's main taxi companies include turquoise-coloured **Dazhong Taxi** (☎ 96822), **Qiangsheng** (☎ 6258 0000) and **Bashi** (☎ 96840).

PRACTICALITIES
BUSINESS HOURS

Banks, offices and government departments are normally open Monday to Friday from 9am to noon and about 2pm to 4.30pm. Most major post offices open daily 8.30am to 6pm, sometimes until 10pm. Bank of China branches are normally open weekdays from 9.30am to 11.30am and 1.30pm to 4.30pm; most have 24-hour ATMs. Some branches also open on Saturday mornings. Shopping malls and department stores are generally open from 10am to 10pm.

Restaurants are open from 11am to 10pm or later, but some close for an afternoon break at

INSIDER TIPS

> Cars can turn corners on red lights, so don't ever assume the green man means you're safe!
> Take your mobile phone with you wherever you go for phoning an English-speaking Shanghai contact who can interpret (p88).
> If you're doing a lot of travelling, buy a transport card (p144) to avoid the long queues in the metro.
> When finding your way, use the Chinese characters in this book to show to locals who will know at a glance what you are after.
> Don't tip taxi drivers.

about 2.30pm before opening again from 5pm to 11pm or later. Some bars open in the morning, others are open from around 5pm to 2am.

HOLIDAYS

Some of the below are nominal holidays and do not qualify for a day off from work:

New Year's Day 1 January
Spring Festival 3 February 2011; 23 January 2012: a week-long break, also known as Chinese New Year
Tomb Sweeping Day First weekend in April; a three-day weekend
International Labour Day 1 May
Dragon Boat Festival 16 June 2010, 6 June 2011
Mid-Autumn Festival 22 September 2010, 12 September 2011
National Day 1 October; officially three days, but often morphs into a week-long holiday

INTERNET

China has the world's largest online population, with almost 300 million internet users in 2009. But the internet is patrolled by Beijing's censors, and sites such as Google or YouTube will sporadically go down. Most midrange and top-end hotels provide broadband internet access, for which there may be a charge. A growing number of hotels, restaurants, bars and cafes now provide wireless access. Hourly rates at internet cafes start from around Y2 to Y3 per hour, and they are typically open 24 hours or 8am to midnight. Take your passport for ID. The easiest way to find the nearest internet cafe is to show the characters 网吧 to someone.

Eastday B@r (东方网点; Map pp64–5, D2; 24 E Ruijin No 2 Rd; 瑞金东二路24号; per hr Y3; ☺ 8am-2am)
Highland Internet Café (智高点网吧; Map pp40–1, E3; 4th fl, Mankedun Guangchang, E Nanjing Rd; 南京东路曼克顿广场4楼; per hr Y3; ☺ 24hr)
Jidu Kongjian Internet Café (极度空间网吧; Map pp64–5, B2; cnr N Xiangyang Rd & Changle Rd; 襄阳北路、长乐路交叉口; per hr Y3; ☺ 24hr)
Xuandong Internet Café (炫动网吧; Map pp84–5, D6; 4th fl, W Nanjing Rd; 南京西路; per hr Y3; ☺ 24hr) Opposite the Children's Palace.

USEFUL WEBSITES

City Weekend (www.cityweekend.com.cn/shanghai) Comprehensive listings website.
CTrip (www.english.ctrip.com) Discounted hotels and air tickets; recommended.
Shanghai Daily (www.shanghaidaily.com) Local news.
Shanghaiist (www.shanghaiist.com) News, gossip, blogs, forum.
Smart Shanghai (www.smartshanghai.com) Events, listings, entertainment ticketing.

LANGUAGE

The official language of the People's Republic of China is Putonghua, based on (but not identical to) the Beijing Mandarin dialect. The local dialect of Shanghai is Shanghainese, although everyone also speaks Mandarin.

Written Chinese script is based on ancient pictograph characters that have been simplified over time; while more than 56,000 characters have been verified, it is commonly held that a well-educated Chinese person knows and uses between 6000 and 8000 characters. Pinyin has been developed as a Romanisation of Mandarin using English letters, but many Shanghainese cannot read it. In this book we've used a simplified version of Pinyin, ie without the tone marks.

A growing number of Shanghainese speak some English; in tourist hotels and restaurants and at major sights you'll get along OK without Mandarin. But if you venture into shops, neighbourhoods or conversations that are off the tourist track, you may find yourself lost for words. Names and addresses are provided in Chinese characters throughout this book to use when you're taking taxis. It's also useful to have the concierge of your hotel write down your address in Chinese before you go anywhere.

For a user-friendly guide, with pronunciation tips and a comprehensive phrase list (including script that you can simply show to people rather than speak), get a copy of Lonely Planet's *Mandarin* phrasebook.

BASICS

See also the Quick Reference section on the inside front cover.

Hello.
Ni hao.
你好。

Goodbye.
Zaijian.
再见。

Please.
Qing.
请。

Thank you.
Xiexie.
谢谢。

Yes.
Shide.
是的。

No. (don't have)
Mei you.
没有。

No. (not so)
Bushi.
不是。

Do you speak English?
Ni hui shuo Yingyu ma?
你会说英语吗？

Do you understand?
Dong ma?
懂吗？

I understand.
Wo tingdedong.
我听得懂。

Could you please ...?
Ni neng buneng ...?
你能不能...？

repeat that
chongfu
重复

speak more slowly
shuo man dianr
说慢点儿

write it down
xie xialai
写下来

EATING & DRINKING

I don't want MSG.
Wo bu yao weijing.
我不要味精。

I'm vegetarian.
Wo chi su.
我吃素。

Not too spicy.
Buyao taila.
不要太辣。

Let's eat!
Chi fan!
吃饭！

Cheers!
Ganbei!
干杯！

INTERNET

Is there a local internet cafe?
Bendi you wangba ma? 本地有网吧吗？

Where can I get online?
Wo zai nar keyi shangwang? 我在哪儿可以上网？

TRANSPORT

Please use the meter.
Qing da biao. 请打表。

How much (is it) to …?
Qu … duoshao qian? 去…多少钱？

EMERGENCIES

It's an emergency!
Zhe shi jinji qingkuang!
这是紧急情况！

Could you help me, please?
Ni neng buneng bang wo ge mang?
你能不能帮我个忙？

Call the police/a doctor/an ambulance!
Qing jiao jingcha/yisheng/jiuhuche!
请叫警察/医生/救护车！

Where's the police station?
Paichusuo zai nar?
派出所在哪儿？

NUMBERS

1	*yi/yao*	一
2	*er/liang*	二/两
3	*san*	三
4	*si*	四
5	*wu*	五
6	*liu*	六
7	*qi*	七
8	*ba*	八
9	*jiu*	九
10	*shi*	十
20	*ershi*	二十
30	*sanshi*	三十

MENU DECODER

>	menu	*caidan*	菜单
>	bill (cheque) please	*maidan/ jiezhang*	买单/ 结账
>	rice	*baifan/ mifan*	白饭/ 米饭
>	noodles	*miantiao*	面条
>	salt	*yan*	盐
>	pepper	*hujiao*	胡椒
>	sugar	*tang*	糖
>	soy sauce	*jiangyou*	酱油
>	beef	*niurou*	牛肉
>	pork	*zhurou*	猪肉
>	chicken	*jirou*	鸡肉
>	lamb	*yangrou*	羊肉
>	vegetables	*shucai*	蔬菜
>	potato	*tudou*	土豆
>	broccoli	*xilanhua*	西兰花
>	chopsticks	*kuaizi*	筷子
>	knife	*daozi*	刀子
>	fork	*chazi*	叉子
>	spoon	*shaozi*	勺子

40	*sishi*	四十
50	*wushi*	五十
60	*liushi*	六十
70	*qishi*	七十
80	*bashi*	八十
90	*jiushi*	九十
100	*yibai*	一百
1000	*yiqian*	一千

DAYS

Monday	*xingqiyi*	星期一
Tuesday	*xingqi'er*	星期二
Wednesday	*xingqisan*	星期三
Thursday	*xingqisi*	星期四
Friday	*xingqiwu*	星期五
Saturday	*xingqiliu*	星期六
Sunday	*xingqitian*	星期天

MONEY

ATMs that take foreign cards are widespread; try to stick to the Bank of China (中国银行), the Industrial and Commercial Bank of China (工商银行; ICBC) and HSBC (汇丰银行) ATMs, many of which are 24-hour. Many top-end hotels, shopping malls and department stores also have ATMs.

Shanghai is an expensive destination. Aim to spend upwards of Y500 a day for modest comfort. Accommodation will be your greatest expense, ranging from Y300 for the cheapest midrange room to over Y2000 per night in the best hotels.

Credit cards are generally more accepted in Shanghai than elsewhere in China. Most tourist hotels will accept major credit cards such as Visa, Amex, MasterCard, Diners and JCB, as will banks, upper-end restaurants and tourist-related shops. Smaller shops and hotels could well not accept credit cards, so check. The following are emergency contact numbers in case you lose your card.

American Express (☎ 6279 8082; 🕙 9am-noon & 1-5.30pm) Out of business hours call the 24-hour refund line in Hong Kong (☎ 852-2811 6122).
MasterCard (☎ 108-00-110 7309)
Visa (☎ 108-00-110 2911)

CURRENCY

The Chinese currency is known as Renminbi (RMB). The basic unit of

HAGGLING

Haggling in markets is standard procedure. Come in at around 30% to 40% of the asking price, or lower. Don't argue, keep smiling and simply walk away if you think the price is too high. Vendors will typically punch a price into a calculator, wave it in your face before factoring it down till you agree on a price. Compare prices at stalls and see how low vendors will go. If goods are faked, then pay fake prices: at some markets you can get up to 80% off the asking price for fake goods, so come in low.

RMB is the yuan (Y), divided into 10 *jiao*. In spoken Chinese the yuan is referred to as *kuai* and *jiao* as *mao*. Bills appear in denominations of one, two, five, 10, 20, 50 and 100 yuan. Coins come in denominations of one *yuan,* five and one *jiao*.

NEWSPAPERS AND MAGAZINES

Look out for the glossy bimonthly *City Weekend* (www.cityweekend .com.cn) and the monthly *That's Shanghai* (www.urbanatomy.com) for comprehensive cultural info and entertainment listings.

ORGANISED TOURS

Shanghai Sideways (www.shanghaiside ways.com) provides one-of-a-kind motorcycle sidecar tours of the city. Night-time bike tours (Y150) are available via **BOHDI** (www.bohdi.com.cn) on Tuesday and Thursday and **SISU** (www.sisucycling.com) on Wednesday.

....

TELEPHONE

COUNTRY & CITY CODES

Note the following country and city codes:

People's Republic of China (☎ 86)
Beijing (☎ 010)
Shanghai (☎ 021)

If calling Shanghai or Beijing from abroad, drop the first zero.

USEFUL PHONE NUMBERS

International directory enquiry (☎ 106)
Shanghai Call Centre (☎ 962 288) English speaking. Operates 24 hours.
Local directory enquiries (☎ 114)

MOBILE PHONES

Ensure your phone is unlocked for use on any network so you can get a Chinese SIM card. Mobile-phone

---

GUANXI

If you want to contact a tourist, entertainment, shopping or business venue in Shanghai and have a mobile phone, then text message the name of the venue to the wireless search engine GuanXi on ☎ 1066 9588 2929. The full name, address and directions, plus telephone number will be immediately returned to you by SMS (Y1 to Y2 per enquiry). The information can also be relayed in Chinese, as long as your mobile phone can support Chinese text.

---

shops – such as China Mobile – sell SIM cards from Y60 to Y100, including Y50 of credit. SIM cards are also available from some newspaper kiosks. Top up credits with a credit-charging card (充值卡; *chongzhi ka*). You can rent a mobile phone (Y40 per day, Y200 per week) at Pudong International Airport, but you'll still need to get a SIM card.

PHONECARDS

Telephone (Integrated Circuit – IC; IC卡) cards can be used for local and (expensive) international calls in public street phones, Telecom offices and most hotels. The internet phonecard (IP card; IP卡), purchased at newspaper kiosks, is much cheaper for international calls; use any home phone, some hotel and some public phones (but not card phones) to dial a special telephone number and follow the instructions. Check you have the right card for use in Shanghai.

....

TIPPING

Tipping is generally not done in Shanghai. Taxi drivers do not expect tips. Don't tip at restaurants (although smarter restaurants will add on a service charge), but feel free to tip hotel porters.

....

TOURIST INFORMATION

Your hotel should be able to provide you with most of the tourist information you require;

badger the concierge for a map of Shanghai. **Tourist Information and Service Centres** (旅游咨询服务中心; http://lyw.sh.gov.cn) are of limited use; some branches have free maps. Locations include the following:

French Concession (Map pp64–5, E2; ☎ 5386 1882; 138 S Chengdu Rd; 成都南路138号; ☉ 9am-8.30pm) Just of Middle Huaihai Rd.

Huangpu (Map pp40–1, E3; ☎ 6357 3718; 518 Jiujiang Rd; 九江路518号; ☉ 9.30am-8pm)

Jing'an (Map pp84–5, D6; ☎ 6248 3259; 1699 W Nanjing Rd; 南京西路1699号; ☉ 9am-5pm)

Pudong (Map p93, B3; ☎ 3878 0202; 1st fl, Superbrand Mall, 168 Lujiazui Rd; 陆家嘴路168号1楼; ☉ 9am-6pm)

Yuyuan Gardens (Map p55, C2; ☎ 6355 5032; 149 Jiujiaochang Rd; 旧校场路149号; ☉ 9am-7pm)

There is also the **Shanghai Information Centre for International Visitors** (Map pp64-5, F2; ☎ 6384 9366; Xintiandi South Block, Bldg 2, Lane 123 Xingye Rd; 兴业路123弄2号新天地南里; ☉ 10am-10pm), where you can pick up a map of Xintiandi. The **Tourist Hotline** (☎ 6252 0000; ☉ 9am-8.30pm) offers a limited English-language service.

TRAVELLERS WITH DISABILITIES

Shanghai's traffic, the city's frequent over- and underpasses and widespread indifference to the plight of the wheelchair-bound are the greatest challenges to disabled travellers. There may be 500,000 wheelchair users, but metro system escalators don't go both ways. An increasing number of modern buildings, museums, stadiums and most new hotels are wheelchair accessible.

>INDEX

See also separate subindexes for See (p157), Shop (p158), Eat (p159), Drink (p160) and Play (p160).

A
accommodation 118-19
acrobatics 81, 91
activities, free 33
air travel 143
alleyways 19, 20, 90, 106, 120
antiques 127
architecture 120-1, 140
    art deco 15, 68
    lilong 19, 20, 90, 106, 120
    shikumen 19, 20, 63, 120, 121
art galleries 130, *see also* See subindex
arts 27, 28, 139-40, *see also* film, literature, music
ATMs 150

B
ballroom dancing 90-1
bargaining 150
bars 124-5, *see also* Drink subindex
boat trips 42, 114, 115
books 26, 141-2
Boxer Uprising 137
Buddhist monasteries 107
Bund & People's Square 10-11, 12-13, 38-53, **40-1, 52**
Bund History Museum 42
bus travel 143, 144-5
business hours 146-7

C
cabaret 108
cafes, *see* Eat subindex, Drink subindex

car travel 145
cell phones 88, 151
Chen Liangyu 140
Chiang Kaishek 137
China Shanghai International Arts Festival 28
Chinese New Year 26
Chinese opera 51
churches, *see* See subindex
cinemas 90, 101
classical music, *see* Play subindex
climate change 143
clubs 132, *see also* Play subindex
Communism 10, 86
Confucius Temple 56
costs 150, *see also inside front cover*
credit cards 150
Cultural Revolution 137
CY Tung Maritime Museum 74

D
dancing, ballroom 90-1
day trips 109-15
disabilities, travellers with 152
Dragon Boat Festival 27
drinking 124-5, *see also* Drink subindex
    Bund & People's Square 48-50
    French Concession East 70-1
    French Concession West 79-80

Jing'an 88-90
Old Town 60-1
Pudong 96-7
Duolun Road Cultural Street 106
Du Yuesheng 137

E
economy 139, 140-1
environmental issues 141, 143
etiquette 139
events 25-8
exchange rate, *see inside front cover*
excursions 109-15

F
fashion 126, *see also* Shop subindex
ferries 145
festivals 25-8
film 142
    cinemas 90, 101
    festivals 27
food 122-3, *see also* Shop subindex, Eat subindex
    Bund & People's Square 46-8
    French Concession East 68-70
    French Concession West 78-9
    Hongkou & North Shanghai 108
    Jing'an 87-8
    language 148, 149

food *continued*
  Old Town 59-60
  Pudong 96
  Xujiahui & South
    Shanghai 102-3
Formula 1 racing 27
free activities 33
French Concession East 16-17,
  62-71, **64-5**
French Concession West
  16-17, 72-81, **73**
Fuxing Park 63

G
galleries 130, *see also* See
  subindex
gardens 22, 42, 58, 63,
  112, 115
gay travellers 133
government 140

H
haggling 150
Hangzhou 23, 110-11
history 136-8
holidays 147
Hongkou & North Shanghai
  104-8, **105**
hotels 118-19
Hu Jintao 140

I
internet access 147
internet resources 118, 147
itineraries 29-33

J
Jade Buddha Temple 24, 83
jazz 50, 80-1
Jing'an 82-91, **84-5**
Jing'an Temple 83

K
karaoke 71

L
language 147-9
Lantern Festival 26
lesbian travellers 133
lilong 19, 20, 90, 106, 120
literature 26, 141-2
live music 71, 90, 97
Longhua Temple Fair 26-7
Lu Xun 106,107
Luziajui 14, 92-7, **93**

M
M50 Art Centre 21, 83
magazines 150
Mao Zedong 83, 137
marathons 28
markets 131, *see also* Shop
  subindex
martial arts 129
massages 128
Masters Cup 27
Metersbonwe Costume
  Museum 42
metro system 145-6
Mid-Autumn Festival 27
mobile phones 88, 151
Moller House 16
monasteries 107
money 150
Moon Festival 27
museums, *see* See *subindex*
music 71, *see also* Play
  subindex

N
National Day 27
New Year, Chinese 26
newspapers 150
nightlife 132, *see also* Play
  subindex
North Shanghai 104-8, **105**

O
Old Town 54-61, **55**
opening hours 146-7
opera, Chinese 51

P
parks & gardens 22, 42, 58,
  63, 112, 115
passports 143-4
Peace Hotel 42-3
People's Square 12-13, 38-53,
  40-1
planning 32
political slogans 10
politics 140
pollution 141
Pudong 14, 92-7, **93**

Q
Qibao 100
Qingming Festival 26

R
religion 134
restaurants, *see* Eat *subindex*
river cruises 42, 114, 115
Riverside Promenade 94

S
safety 59
scams 43, 59
Shanghai Art Museum 43
Shanghai Biennale 27
Shanghai Gallery of Art 43
Shanghai Grand Theatre 50
Shanghai History Museum
  94
Shanghai International Film
  Festival 27
Shanghai International
  Literary Festival 26
Shanghai International
  Marathon 28
Shanghai Museum 12-13, 43

Shanghai Museum of Contemporary Art (MOCA) 43
Shanghai Museum of Folk Collectibles 56
shikumen 19, 20, 63, 120, 121
shopping, *see also* Shop *subindex*
   antiques 127
   Bund & People's Square 44
   fashion 126
   French Concession East 66-8
   French Concession West 75-7
   Hongkou & North Shanghai 107
   itineraries 32
   Jing'an 86-7
   markets 131
   Old Town 58-9
   Pudong 96
   silk 127
   Xujiahui & South Shanghai 101
silk 127
slogans 10
Song Qingling 75
South Shanghai 98-103, **99**
spa treatments 128
sports 27, 28, 129
Spring Festival 26
subway system 145-6
Sun Yatsen 66
Suzhou 23, 112-13
synagogues 106-7

T
taichi 129
Taikang Road Art Centre 18, 66
Taiping Rebellion 136
taxis 146

tea 60-1, 67, 110, 112
telephone services 151
temples, *see* See *subindex*
tennis 27
Tianzifang, *see* Taikang Road Art Centre
tipping 151
Tomb-Sweeping Festival
Tongli 115
tourist information 88, 151-2
tours 150-1
train travel 143, 145-6
travel passes 144

V
vacations 147
visas 143-4

W
walks 51-3, 107, 110, **52**
West Lake 110-11
World Expo 61

X
Xintiandi 19, 66, 68
Xujiahui & South Shanghai 98-103, **99**

Y
Yuyuan Bazaar 22, 59
Yuyuan Gardens 22, 58

Z
Zhujiajiao 114

Tianzifang 18, 66
Xintiandi 19, 66

Boat Trips
Huangpu River Cruise 42
Tongli 115
Zhujiajiao 114

Churches & Cathedrals
Catholic Church 100
Hongkew Methodist Church 106
St Ignatius Cathedral 101
St Nicholas Church 66
Zhujiajiao Catholic Church of Ascension 114

Galleries
Art Labor 66
Contrasts 39
James Cohan 66
M50 Art Centre 21, 83
Propaganda Poster Art Centre 74-5
Shanghai Art Museum 43
Shanghai Gallery of Art 43
Shanghai Museum of Contemporary Art (MOCA) 43
ShanghARt 63
Taikang Rd Art Centre 18, 66
Tianzifang 18, 66
Zendai Museum of Modern Art 96

Monasteries
Xiahai Buddhist Monastery 107

Museums
Bund History Museum 42
Bund Museum 39
China Tea Museum 110
Chinese Medicine Museum 110

◉ SEE

Areas & Streets
Duolun Road Cultural Street 106
Riverside Promenade 94
Qinghefang Old Street 110
Taikang Road Art Centre 18, 66

INDEX

Chinese Sex Museum 115
CY Tung Maritime Museum 74
Fisherman's Wharf 106
Lu Xun Memorial Hall 106
Metersbonwe Costume
   Museum 42
Post Museum 107
Shadow Puppet Museum
   100
Shanghai Art Museum 43
Shanghai History Museum 94
Shanghai Museum 12-13, 43
Shanghai Museum of Arts &
   Crafts 75
Shanghai Museum of
   Contemporary Art (MOCA) 43
Shanghai Museum of Folk
   Collectibles 56
Shanghai Urban Planning
   Exhibition Hall 44
Shikumen Open House
   Museum 63
Suzhou Museum 112
Suzhou Silk Museum 112
Zendai Museum of Modern
   Art 96

Notable Buildings
Bank of China building 39
Bibliotheca Zi-Ka-Wei 100
Chenxiangge Nunnery 56
Dajing Pavilion 56
former residence of Mao
   Zedong 83
Gengle Tang 115
Guanyin Tower 56
Hongkong & Shanghai
   Banking Corporation (HSBC)
   building 42

Jinmao Tower 94
Moller House 16
Oriental Pearl TV Tower 94
Peace Hotel 42-3
Pearl Pagoda 115
Shanghai Children's Palace
   86
Shanghai World Financial
   Center 94-6
site of the 1st National
   Congress of the CCP 63-6
Song Qingling's former
   residence 75
Sun Yatsen's former
   residence 66
Ward Road Jail 107

Parks & Gardens
Fuxing Park 63
Garden of the Master of the
   Nets 112
Huangpu Park 42
Humble Administrator's
   Garden 112
Tuisi Garden 115
Yuyuan Gardens 22, 58

Synagogues
Ohel Moishe Synagogue
   106-7

Temples
Baopu Taoist Temple 110
Baochu Pagoda 110
City God Temple 114
Confucius Temple 56
Jade Buddha Temple 24, 83
Jing'an Temple 83
Leifeng Pagoda 110
Lingyin Temple 110
Longhua Temple & Pagoda
   100-1
North Temple Pagoda 112

Temple of Mystery 112
Temple of the Town God
   56-8
West Garden Temple 112
Yuanjin Buddhist Temple
   114

SHOP
Art & Antiques
Art Deco 86
Dongtai Road Antique
   Market 58
Fuyou Antique Market 58
Madame Mao's Dowry 77
Shanghai Museum Art
   Store 44

Body & Bath Products
Ba Yan Ka La 75

Ceramics
Blue Shanghai White 44
Spin 77

Electronics
Cybermart 67

Fabric
Chinese Printed Blue Nankeen
   Exhibition Hall 77
Shiliupu Fabric Market 59
Silk King 127
Wangjia Docks Fabric
   Market 59

Fashion
Annabel Lee 44
AP Xinyang Fashion & Gifts
   Market 96
Cool Docks 58
Elbis Hungi 75
eno 75
Fenshine Fashion &
   Accessories Plaza 86-7

000 map pages

Heping Finery 67
Insh 67
Junmeizu 75
One by One 75
Qipu Market 107
Shanghai Tang 67
Shiatzy Chen 44-6
Shiliupu Fabric Market 59
Shirt Flag 67
Source 75
Taikang Road Art Centre 18, 68
Thing 75
Urban Tribe 77
Xintiandi 19, 68

Food & Tea
Shanghai No 1 (First) Food Store 44
Huifeng Tea Shop 67

Handicrafts
Brocade Country 75-7
Skylight 77
Springhead 68

Home Decor
Simply Life 77

Malls
Grand Gateway 101

Markets
AP Xinyang Fashion & Gifts Market 96
Dongtai Road Antique Market 58
Fuyou Antique Market 58
Qipu Market 107
Shiliupu Fabric Market 59
Wangjia Docks Fabric Market 59
Yuyuan Bazaar 22, 59

Pearls
Amy Lin's Pearls & Jewellery 86

Shoes
100 Change & Insect 67
Suzhou Cobblers 46

Souvenirs
AP Xinyang Fashion & Gifts Market 96
Madame Mao's Dowry 77
Old Street 58
Shanghai Museum Art Store 44
Taikang Road Art Centre 18, 68
Xintiandi 19, 68
Yunhong Chopsticks Shop 46
Yuyuan Bazaar 22, 59

🍴 EAT
Cafes
Ginger 78
Kommune 69

Chinese
Gongdelin 46
Shanghai Grandmother 47
Songyuelou 60
Tiandi 48
Vegetarian Lifestyle 70, 88
Xindalu 108

Continental
M on the Bund 46-7

Dim Sum
Crystal Jade 68-9

Dumplings
Din Tai Fung 69
Nanxiang Steamed Bun Restaurant 60
Yang's Fry Dumplings 48

Food Courts
Dragon Gate Mall 59-60
On 56 96
Superbrand Mall 96

Food Streets
Nan Dajie 100
Yunnan Road Food Street 48

Fusion
Azul 78
Factory 108
Jean Georges 46
T8 70
Vargas Grill 78
Viva 78

Hotpots
Donglaishun 102
Qimin Organic Hotpot 88

Hunanese
Di Shui Dong 69
South Memory 47

Indonesian
Bali Laguna 87

Japanese
Haiku 78

Manchurian
Dongbei Ren 69

Noodles
Ajisen 48
Noodle Bull 79
Wuyue Renjia 48

Shanghainese
Bai's Restaurant 78
Baoluo Jiulou 78
Fu 1039 87
Jishi Jiulou 78-9
Lynn 88
Ye Olde Station Restaurant 103
Ye Shanghai 70

Sichuanese
Pinchuan 79
Sichuan Citizen 79
South Beauty 96

Uighur
Uighur Restaurant 70, 102

Vegetarian
Vegetarian Lifestyle 70, 88

Yunnanese
Lost Heaven 79
Southern Barbarian 69

Y DRINK
Bars
100 Century Avenue 96-7
Abbey Road 79
Bar Rouge 48
Barbarossa 48
Big Bamboo 88
Boxing Cat Brewery 80
Captain's Bar 49
Cloud 9 97
Cotton's 80
DR Bar 70
Eddy's Bar 133
Fat Olive 60
Frangipani 133
Glamour Bar 50
Little Face 80
LOgO 80
New Heights 50
TMSK 70-1

Velvet Lounge 80
Zapata's 80

Cafes
Boonna Café 79-80
Bund 12 Café 49
Café 85°C 88-90
Citizen Café 70
Wagas 90

Teahouses
Humble Administrator's
    Garden 112
Old Shanghai Teahouse 60-1

☆ PLAY
Acrobatics
Shanghai Centre Theatre 91
Shanghai Fantasia 81

Ballroom Dancing
Paramount Ballroom 90-1

Cabaret
Chinatown 108

Chinese Opera
Yifu Theatre 51

Cinema
Image Tunnel 90

Classical Music
Shanghai Concert Hall 50
Shanghai Conservatory of
    Music 71
Shanghai Grand Theatre 50

Clubs
Babyface 71
D2 133
Dragon Club 81
M1nt 50
Muse 90
Shanghai Studio 133
Shelter 81
Sin Lounge 91

Jazz
Cabaret 50
Cotton Club 80-1
JZ Club 81

Karaoke
Partyworld 71

Live Music
Bandu Cabin 90
Melting Pot 71
Oriental Art Center 97
Yuyintang 71
Zhijiang Dream Factory 71

Massages & Spa
Treatments
Dragonfly 128
Green Massage 128
Lulu Massage 128

Martial Arts
Longwu Kungfu Center 129
Mingwu International Kungfu
    129
Oz Body Fit 129

000 map pages